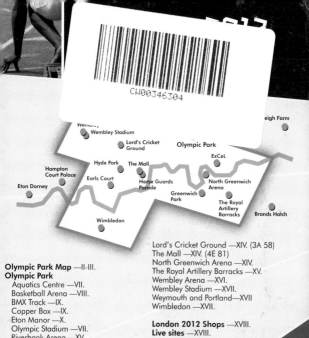

Olympic Park

ExCeL

Wembley Stadium

Lord's Cricket Ground

Wembley

eigh Farm

Hyde Park   The Mall

Hampton Court Palace

Earls Court

Horse Guards Parade

North Greenwich Arena

Eton Dorney

Greenwich Park

The Royal Artillery Barracks

Brands Hatch

Wimbledon

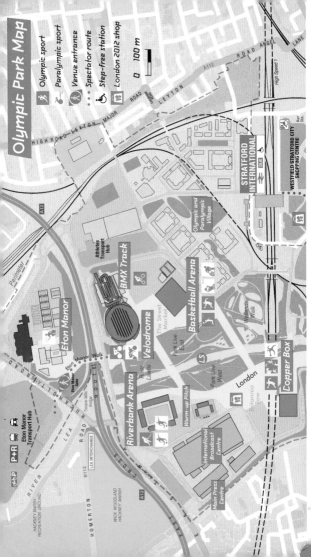

Olympic Park Map

Key:
- Olympic sport
- Paralympic sport
- Venue entrance
- Spectator route
- Step-free station
- London 2012 shop

0   100 m

This summer London and the UK will come alive with the world's largest sporting events when the Games begin.

The London 2012 Olympic and Paralympic Games will encompass 30 days of competition with 14,723 athletes and millions of people gathered here to enjoy the sporting and cultural action.

Olympic Heritage

The first ancient Olympic Games can be traced back to 776 BC. They were dedicated to the Olympian gods and staged on the plains of Olympia in Greece. The modern Olympic Games were founded by French-born athlete, poet and educator Pierre de Coubertin (1863–1937).

Olympic Games

In 2012 London will host a Games like never before, drawing on the UK's proud Olympic heritage. In 1908, London stood in as Host City for Rome after an eruption of Mount Vesuvius. It was the first time that the athletes paraded under national flags at the start of the Games. In 1948, London again stepped in at the last minute to host the first Games after World War II. It was the first time that the Games were shown on home television.

Paralympic Games

The London 2012 Paralympic Games are being organised together with the Olympic Games. In 1948, Dr Ludwig Guttmann organised a sports competition that involved World War II soldiers with spinal cord injuries based at Stoke Mandeville Hospital. The competition took place between sports clubs and other hospitals on the same day as the Opening Ceremony of the London 1948 Olympic Games. Four years later, athletes from Holland joined in, creating the forerunner of the Paralympic Games. The first official Paralympic Games was that held in Rome in 1960.

Olympic Torch Relay

An important element of the Olympic Games of ancient Greece, the Flame is lit from the sun's rays at the Temple of Hera in Olympia. The Olympic Torch Relay route has been planned so that the Flame will come within 10 miles of 95% of people in the UK. The last Torchbearer lights the cauldron at the Olympic Games Opening Ceremony.

Cultural Olympiad

The London 2012 Festival, will bring leading artists from all over the world to create the UK's biggest ever festival; a chance for everyone to celebrate London 2012 through dance, music, theatre, the visual arts, film and digital innovation and leave a lasting legacy for the arts in the UK.

Legacy

For the first time, the Games are being planned hand-in-hand with the long-term improvement of the area. A new sustainable community will be integrated with the area surrounding the Olympic Park, with local people benefiting from a new park, homes and world-class sporting facilities.

Olympic Stadium

The Olympic Stadium will host the Athletics and Paralympic Athletics events at the London 2012 Games, as well as the Opening and Closing Ceremonies.

 ## Athletics

One of the most popular sports is also the biggest, with 2,000 athletes competing in 47 events. There are four main strands to the Athletics competition: track events, such as the 100m; field events, which include the High Jump and the Shot Put; combined events such as the Decathlon, a mix of track and field elements; and road events, among them the Marathon.

Paralympic Athletics

Athletics will also be the largest sport at the Paralympic Games with 1,100 athletes competing. Some athletes compete in wheelchairs or throwing frames, others with prostheses, and others with the guidance of a sighted companion.

Aquatics Centre

The Aquatics Centre will be the venue for Swimming, Paralympic Swimming, Diving, Synchronised Swimming and the swimming element of the Modern Pentathlon. The venue features a spectacular wave-like roof that is 160m long and up to 80m wide.

Diving

Diving requires acrobatic excellence and supreme coordination skills, as athletes dive from heights of up to 10m.

Swimming

There are four strokes used in Olympic competition: Freestyle, Backstroke, Breaststroke and Butterfly. The 10km Marathon Swimming will be held in the Serpentine within Hyde Park.

Synchronised Swimming

Synchronised Swimmers use pinpoint precision and immense stamina to deliver beautiful routines in the pool.

Modern Pentathlon

The venue for the swimming element of Modern Pentathlon. The fencing element takes place in Copper Box, riding and the combined event will be staged in Greenwich Park.

Paralympic Swimming

Swimmers are classified according to their functional ability to perform each stroke, and compete against athletes in their own classification.

The fourth-largest venue on the Olympic Park and one of the largest ever temporary venues built for any Games.

Basketball

Preliminaries and women's quarter-finals are held here at the Basketball Arena. All other rounds take place in the North Greenwich Arena.

Handball

Venue for the Handball men's quarter-finals, all semi-finals and all medal matches. All other rounds take place in the Copper Box.

Wheelchair Basketball

Preliminary games will be split between the Basketball Arena and North Greenwich Arena. All quarter-finals, semi-finals and medal games will take place at North Greenwich Arena.

Wheelchair Rugby

Played indoors on a regulation-size basketball court by teams of four, contact between wheelchairs is permitted, but physical contact is outlawed.

BMX Track

The purpose built BMX Track will be reconfigured after the Games to form part of a new VeloPark with a mountain bike track and road-cycle circuit.

BMX Racing

Inspired by motocross, BMX Racing is the most recent discipline to have been added to the Olympic programme.

Brands Hatch

Brands Hatch motor racing circuit in Kent is approximately 20 miles south-east of the Olympic Park.

Paralympic Cycling - Road

Athletes with a visual impairment, cerebral palsy, amputations or other physical disabilities compete on bicycles, tricycles, tandems and hand cycles.

Copper Box

This Olympic Park venue will be adapted after the Games to become a multi-use sports centre for community use, athlete training and small- to medium-sized events.

Handball

Preliminary rounds of both the men's and women's competitions, as well as the women's quarter-finals, will take place here. The competition will then move to the Basketball Arena, also in the Olympic Park.

Modern Pentathlon

Fencing, the first element of Modern Pentathlon takes place here. Swimming takes place in the Aquatics Centre, riding and the combined event will be staged in Greenwich Park.

Goalball

Goalball is played by visually impaired athletes using a ball with bells inside. Athletes wear blackout masks on the playing court, which allows persons with varying degrees of vision to participate together.

Earls Court

A major west London venue for exhibitions, conferences and events. It first opened its doors in 1937, and now holds hundreds of events each year.

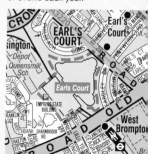

Volleyball

The dynamic, competitive sport of Volleyball made its Olympic Games debut in 1964.

Eton Dorney

Eton Dorney is located near Windsor Castle, about 25 miles west of London.

 ## Canoe Sprint

Races will be held over three distances with the fastest races taking just 30 seconds to complete. Canoe Slalom takes place at Lee Valley White Water Centre.

 ## Rowing

The 14 Olympic Rowing events range from the Single Sculls, featuring solo rowers, to the Eights, contested by teams of eight rowers plus a cox.

 ## Paralympic Rowing

Appearing at the Paralympic Games for only the second time. Adaptive rowing boats are equipped with special seats, which vary according to the disability of the athlete.

Eton Manor

Eton Manor will be transformed after the Games into sporting facilities for local and regional communities.

 ## Wheelchair Tennis

First played in 1976, Wheelchair Tennis is one of the fastest-growing wheelchair sports in the world.

ExCeL

A London Docklands exhibition and conference centre, its arenas will host a range of Olympic and Paralympic sports.

 ## Boxing

Men's Boxing events will be joined on the Olympic programme by a women's competition for the first time. Boxing featured at the original Olympic Games in the 7th century BC.

 ## Fencing

Although sword fighting dates back thousands of years, Fencing really came of age as a sport in the 19th century.

Judo

Developed from jujitsu and established as a sport in the late 19th century, contests will be a five-minute whirlwind of combat, with athletes attempting a combination of throws and holds in a bid to defeat their opponents.

 ## Table Tennis

Table tennis, based on the same basic principles as Tennis, is a spectacle that blends power, speed, skill and subtlety.

 ## Taekwondo

'Taekwondo' translates into English as 'the way of foot and fist' – an accurate description of this martial art - with the aim being to land powerful kicks and punches on your opponent.

 ## Weightlifting

The aim of Weightlifting is simple, to lift more weight than anyone else - resulting in pure sporting theatre. The strongest competitors may lift more than three times their body weight.

 ## Wrestling

Recognised as one of the world's oldest sports, Wrestling was first held at the ancient Olympic Games in 708 BC.

 ## Boccia

Boccia is a target sport that tests muscle control and accuracy, demanding extreme skill and concentration. Players must be in a seated position within a throwing box at one end of the playing court.

 ## Paralympic Judo

Contested by visually impaired athletes, the mats have different textures to indicate the competition area and zones.

 ## Paralympic Table Tennis

A permanent part of the Paralympic programme since the first Games in 1960, it is also one of the largest with 29 medal events and 300 athletes.

 ## Powerlifting

Powerlifting is a bench-press competition – competitors are classified by bodyweight alone.

 ## Sitting Volleyball

Sitting Volleyball emerged in the Netherlands in the 1950s, a combination of Volleyball and a German game called Sitzbal.

 ## Wheelchair Fencing

Athletes compete in wheelchairs fastened to the floor, resulting in a fierce, fast-moving battle of tactics and technique.

Greenwich Park

Greenwich Park will host the Olympic and Paralympic Equestrian competitions, plus the combined running and shooting element of the Modern Pentathlon. Situated on the south bank of the River Thames in south-east London.

Equestrian - Dressage

Dressage events will be a test of both athletic prowess and supreme elegance.

Equestrian - Eventing

Featuring dressage, cross-country and a dramatic jumping finale, the Eventing competition showcases an all-encompassing test of Equestrian skill.

Equestrian - Jumping

Known as 'show jumping' in the UK, the Jumping competition will require horse and rider to navigate a short course with precision, speed and perfect technique.

Modern Pentathlon

Riding and combined running/shooting will be staged here in Greenwich Park. Fencing will be in the Copper Box, swimming in the Aquatics Centre - both venues in the Olympic Park.

Paralympic Equestrian

Athletes with a disability have long taken part in Equestrian activities, originally as a means of rehabilitation and recreation. Classified across five grades to ensure that the tests can be judged on the skill of the rider, regardless of their disability.

Hadleigh Farm

Hadleigh Farm, with its ideal mountain biking terrain, is to the east of London in Essex.

Cycling - Mountain Bike

Rocky paths, tricky climbs and technical descents will provide plenty of challenges for riders in the competition.

Hampton Court Palace

Hampton Court Palace is one of London's historic Royal Palaces. It is located in the London Borough of Richmond upon Thames in south-west London.

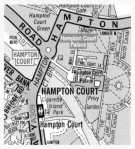

 ### Cycling - Road

The Olympic Road Cycling programme includes two events. Time Trials begin and finish at Hampton Court Palace, Road Racing will begin and end on The Mall.

Horse Guards Parade

Horse Guards Parade is situated between Whitehall and St James's Park. A temporary beach will be created with 3,000 tonnes of imported sand.

 ### Beach Volleyball

Beach Volleyball is similar to the indoor game, although it is played by teams of two, instead of teams of six.

Hyde Park

Within London's West End this extensive park abuts Mayfair and Knightsbridge.

 ### Marathon Swimming 10km

This event takes place in the Serpentine lake. All other swimming events are held in the Olympic Park Aquatics Centre.

Triathlon

Triathlon races combine swimming, cycling and running, in that order. Events are conducted over a variety of distances: for the Olympic Games, the men's and women's Triathlons will consist of a 1,500m swim, a 40km bike ride and a 10km run.

Lee Valley White Water Centre

Lee Valley White Water Centre is located in the River Lee Country Park 30km north of the Olympic Park. After the Games this new centre will become a venue for canoeing, kayaking and white water rafting.

Canoe Slalom

Modelled on slalom skiing, the sport was first staged on flat water, but was later switched to white water rapids. The competitions consist of timed runs down a white water course with up to 25 gates. Canoe Sprint takes place at Eton Dorney.

Lord's Cricket Ground

Lord's is the home of cricket. It is located in St John's Wood, north-west London, near Regent's Park.

 ## Archery

Archery dates back around 10,000 years; developed as a competitive activity in medieval England, it is now practised in more than 140 countries around the world.

The Mall

This famous ceremonial route connects Buckingham Palace and Trafalgar Square.

 ## Athletics - Marathon and Race Walk

The start and finish points for the Olympic Marathon and Race Walk. At London 1908, the marathon distance was extended from around 25 miles to 26.2 miles (42.195 kilometres) so that it finished in front of the Royal Box. This distance became standard for the Marathon and is still used today.

 ## Cycling - Road Racing

The start and finish point for Cycling Road Racing events. There are two Road Cycling events for both men and women. Time Trials take place at Hampton Court Palace.

 ## Paralympic Athletics - Marathon

Men's and women's Marathons will be held on the streets of central London, starting and finishing on The Mall.

North Greenwich Arena

Built for the Millennium celebrations, and transformed into a sports and entertainment venue, the arena is sited on the south side of the River Thames.

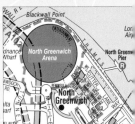

 ## Basketball

Men's quarter-finals and women's semi-finals onwards are held here, preliminaries and women's quarter-finals are held at the Basketball Arena in the Olympic Park.

Gymnastics - Artistic

The grace, strength and skill of Olympic gymnasts have been astonishing audiences since the Games in ancient Greece.

Gymnastics - Trampoline

Trampoline is the newest of the three Gymnastics disciplines making its Olympic debut at Sydney in 2000.

Wheelchair Basketball

Preliminary games will be split between the Olympic Park Basketball Arena and North Greenwich Arena. All quarter-finals, semi-finals and medal games will take place here.

Riverbank Arena

The Riverbank Arena is located in the Olympic Park.

Hockey

Until the 1970s, hockey was always played on grass. However, top-level matches now take place on water-based synthetic-turf pitches.

Paralympic 5-a-side Football

Played by visually impaired athletes plus a sighted goal-keeper using a ball with a noise-making device inside, the pitch is surrounded by a rebound wall. The sport is played with no throw-ins and no offside rule.

Paralympic 7-a-side Football

Follows modified FIFA rules; the playing field is smaller, as are the goals. Teams are made up of ambulant cerebral palsy athletes, featuring players with varying levels of disability.

The Royal Artillery Barracks

Located south of the River Thames in Woolwich, the Barracks are a historic military site dating from 1776.

Shooting

Olympic Shooting events fall broadly into three types: Pistol, Rifle and Shotgun events. The sport of Shooting has been practised competitively for centuries.

Paralympic Archery

Paralympic Archery consists of both standing and wheelchair events for individuals and teams.

Paralympic Shooting

Athletes with different disabilities compete together in two classes – for athletes who can support the weight of their firearm themselves, and for athletes who use a shooting stand to support their arm.

Velodrome

Purpose built within the Olympic Park the Velodrome features a distinctive sweeping roof design reflecting the geometry of the cycling track. After the Games a new mountain bike course and road-cycle circuit will be added to create a VeloPark for the local community, sports clubs and elite athletes.

 Cycling - Track

Cycling has a long history in the UK. As early as 1870, large crowds were drawn to races held on indoor wooden tracks. Track Cycling has featured at every Games but one since the first modern Olympic Games in 1896. There are ten Olympic Track Cycling events (five for men, five for women): Sprint, Keirin, Team Sprint, Team Pursuit and Omnium.

 Paralympic Cycling - Track

The competition is for athletes with a visual impairment, cerebral palsy, amputations or other physical disabilities competing on bicycles, tricycles, tandems and hand cycles.

Water Polo Arena

A temporary Olympic Park venue adjacent to the Aquatics Centre.

 Water Polo

Water Polo developed during the 19th century as an aquatic version of rugby, played informally in rivers and lakes. The version of the game that survives today is closer to handball.

Wembley Arena

A flagship live music and sport venue, in north-west London.

 Badminton

One of the most dynamic Olympic sports, Badminton made its full Olympic debut at Barcelona 1992.

 Gymnastics - Rhythmic

Rhythmic Gymnastics is a combination of gymnastics and dance. Scores are awarded for difficulty, artistry and execution.

XVI

Wembley Stadium

England's national stadium is situated in north-west London, it is the biggest of the six stadiums staging the London 2012 Olympic Games Football competition.

Football

The five other co-Host City stadia are: **City of Coventry Stadium**, Glasgow's **Hampden Park**, Cardiff's **Millennium Stadium**, Manchester's **Old Trafford** and Newcastle upon Tyne's **St. James' Park**. The finals for both the men's and women's competitions will be played at Wembley.

Weymouth and Portland

This beautiful bay setting has some of the best natural sailing waters in the UK.

Sailing

The competition will host 10 Sailing events featuring a variety of craft from dinghies and keelboats, to windsurfing boards.

Paralympic Sailing

Paralympic Sailing will consist of three mixed events.

Wimbledon

The home of the All England Lawn Tennis and Croquet Club. Wimbledon staged the tennis competition for London's first Olympic Games in 1908.

Tennis

The Tennis competition will feature five medal events including Mixed Doubles, making its first apperance since 1924. Situated in south-west London about 12 miles from the Olympic Park.

London 2012 Shops

Canary Wharf, Jubilee Place,
(Off Bank St.)

Heathrow Airport
Terminal 3 (airside)
Terminal 5 (airside)

Hyde Park........................5C 78

John Lewis
Brent Cross Shopping Centre
Kingston, Wood Street
Oxford Street (fifth floor)
....................................5C 68
Stratford City Shopping Centre

Paddington Station............4F 65

Peter Jones, Sloane Square
....................................5E 91

Royal Opera House..........5C 70

St Pancras International.....2B 62

Stansted Airport, Essex

Team GB and ParalympicsGB
Shop: Stratford City Shopping
Centre

http://shop.london2012.com

Live Sites

Live Sites are big screen and
event spaces in urban centres
providing a unique combination
of free sports screenings, cultural
entertainment and ticketed
concerts.

With the exception of the Hyde
Park Opening and Closing
Ceremony Celebrations (27 July
and 12 August), entry will be
free though ticketed to control
numbers, with daily guaranteed
entry tickets available in
advance.
All tickets via btlondonlive.com

BT London Live Sites:
Hyde Park (Olympic Games)
....................................5C 7
Trafalgar Square (Paralympic
Games)....................3A 8:
Victoria Park (Olympic Games)
Additional Live Sites include:
London Park (Olympic Games
& Paralympic Games)
....................................4C 8

Transport

**Scan for up-to-date travel
details and bookings**

**www.london2012.com/
getting-to-the-games**
London 2012 is aiming for a
'public transport' Games, so
please do not drive as there will
be no parking at or around
venues. You can travel to each
competition venue using different types of public transport, or
by walking or cycling.

Venues in London
London's transport system will b
very busy, so you should allow
plenty of time to travel to, from
and between venues. Check the
information on travelling to you

event to find out where your venue is, the best way to get there and how long your journey will take between the recommended stations serving venues. London is well-served by public transport with travel options including the London Underground, London Overground, Docklands Light Railway, National Rail, buses and river services.

Outer London venues
Some sporting events are being held in venues on the outskirts of London, including Eton Dorney, the Lee Valley White Water Centre and Hadleigh Farm. All of these venues are linked to London by National Rail services.

Co-Host Cities and Towns
The co-Host Cities are Cardiff, Coventry, Glasgow, Manchester, Newcastle upon Tyne (all for Football) and Weymouth and Portland (Sailing). They all have National Rail stations with direct links to London, although some of these venues are significant distances from the capital.

Travel tickets
London 2012 ticket holders can benefit from a range of special travel tickets for the Games. Spectators with a ticket for a Games event in London will receive a one-day Games Travelcard for the day of that event, valid within zones 1 to 9. This includes London Underground (Tube), London Overground, Docklands Light Railway (DLR), buses, trams and National Rail services, including the Javelin® service between St Pancras and Stratford

International stations, but excluding the Heathrow, Stansted or Gatwick Express trains, or taxis and private hire vehicles.

Travel to outer London venues
Spectators with tickets for Games events at Eton Dorney, the Lee Valley White Water Centre and Hadleigh Farm will receive a Games Travelcard for use on public transport in London and National Rail between London and the recommended stations for those venues.

London Underground
The Underground is one of the main ways to travel around London. All of the London 2012 venues within London can be reached by London Underground, with the exception of ExCeL, Greenwich Park and The Royal Artillery Barracks. Travel within zones 1 to 9 on London Underground for the day of your event is included with the Games Travelcard. Many of London Underground's stations have been improved to make them more accessible; details on www.tfl.gov.uk

London Buses
London has an extensive bus network and there are routes

Improvement works may affect your journey, please check before you travel

O Interchange stations
Ⓐ Step-free access from street to train
Ⓐ Step-free access from street to platform

Website
tfl.gov.uk

24 hour travel information
0843 222 1234*

*You pay no more than 5p per minute if calling from a BT landline. There may be a connection charge. Charges from mobiles or other landline providers may be higher.

MAYOR OF LONDON

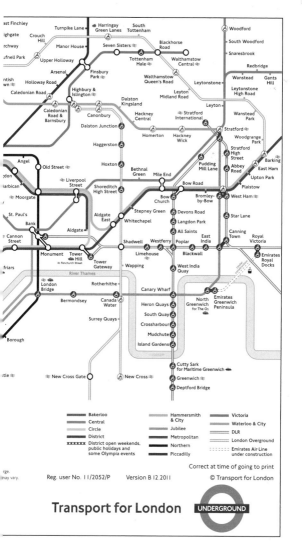

Transport for London   UNDERGROUND

and stops close to all London 2012 venues. London's buses are a good travel option for people with accessibility needs. Most of London's 8,000 buses are low-floor with clearly marked priority seating next to doors for disabled people. There is room for one wheelchair space and assistance dogs are allowed on all buses.

Travel on London's buses on the day of your event is included with the Games Travelcard. There are 24-hour bus routes providing travel options all night in London.

Docklands Light Railway (DLR)

The DLR serves London 2012 venues at the Olympic Park, ExCeL, Greenwich Park and The Royal Artillery Barracks. The DLR is a step-free network and all DLR stations have lift or ramp access to all platforms. Travel on the DLR for the day of your event is included with the Games Travelcard.

London Overground

London Overground is a suburban network of rail services in London, managed by Transport for London. Travel on London Overground on the day of your event is included with the Games Travelcard. Passengers requiring assistance are recom-

mended to give at least 24 hours notice by calling London Overground Customer Services on 0845 601 4867, 9am–5pm on weekdays.

Rail

The National Rail network connects London and all the co-Host Cities for the London 2012 venues. Extra Rail services will be provided to Games venues, and trains will run later from London to key destinations up to approximately two hours away, such as Birmingham, Manchester, Leeds and Cardiff.

Cycling

Cycling in London is an easy and convenient alternative to public transport. Free, secure, managed cycle parking will be provided at all London 2012 venues. Bicycle locks are not supplied. TfL cycle hire docking stations may be within walking distance of London 2012 venues, but you will not be able to dock your cycle hire bike at venues.

Shuttle Buses

Shuttle buses will be provided from some recommended stations to London 2012 and co-Host City venues, particularly where these stations are more than a short walk away from the venue entrance. These shuttles will be low-floor accessible buses and the service will be available for all spectators.

River services

Venues accessible by river include Greenwich Park, North Greenwich Arena, The Royal Artillery Barracks, Horse Guards

Parade, The Mall and Eton Dorney. All passengers on boat services will have a seat or wheelchair space. Travel by scheduled river services on the Thames in London is not included with the Games Travelcard provided with your event tickets, but it does entitle spectators to a one third discount on the price of river service tickets.

Taxis
Taxis and private hire vehicles do not accept Oyster cards or travelcards and are not covered by the Games Travelcard that you will receive with your event ticket.

Only licensed taxis can pick up passengers on the street or at ranks without a booking. Minicabs and other private hire vehicles must be booked through a licensed operator (in person, over the phone or online) before the journey starts. Unbooked minicabs are illegal. You may be approached by touts or minicab drivers seeking passengers or offering a service; these are unsafe, unlicensed and uninsured. You put yourself in danger if you use these services.

2012 Games coach services
- During the Olympic Games coach services will be provided to the Olympic Park, ExCeL, Greenwich Park (30 July only) and Weymouth and Portland from a range of locations outside the M25. Coaches will pick up from bus stops and bus stations throughout Great Britain.
- During the Paralympic Games, 2012 Games coach services will be provided to the Olympic Park and ExCeL.
- All passengers on the coach services will have a dedicated seat or wheelchair space.
- All seats and wheelchair spaces on 2012 Games coach services must be booked in advance: www.firstgroupgames travel.com/direct-coaching

2012 Games park-and-ride
- Secure park-and-ride sites with limited space will be provided at convenient locations.
- Park-and-ride services must be booked in advance: www.firstgroupgamestravel.com
- Venues with park-and-ride facilities during the Olympic Games include: the Olympic Park, ExCeL, Greenwich Park (30 July only), Eton Dorney, Hadleigh Farm, the Lee Valley White Water Centre and Weymouth and Portland.
- Venues with park-and-ride facilities during the Paralympic Games include: the Olympic Park, ExCeL, and Eton Dorney.

Blue Badge Parking
Blue Badge parking spaces are available for spectators who hold a valid Blue Badge or recognised national disability permit.
- Blue Badge parking spaces must be booked in advance: www.firstgroupgamestravel.com

Scan for 2012 Games spectator journey planner

Plan your journey using the 2012 Games spectator journey planner. It will provide you with:
- Estimated journey times to and from Games venues from anywhere in Great Britain.
- Estimated walking and cycling times to and from recommended stations to Games venues.
- Timetable information to allow Games ticket holders to plan their travel.
- Links to travel booking sites (such as 2012 Games Rail services and 2012 Games coach services) to enable Games ticket holders to purchase travel tickets in advance of travel.
- Recommended routes to make your journey as easy as possible.

Useful websites

London 2012 Information
www.london2012.com
2012 Games Travel Services
Rail:
■ www.nationalrailgames
  travel.co.uk
Eurostar:
■ www.eurostar.com

Coach, park-and-ride & Blue Badge:
■ www.firstgroupgames
  travel.co.uk
River:
■ www.citycruisesgames
  travel.co.uk
■ https://booking.thames
  clippers.com/gamestravel

■ www.frenchbrothers.co.uk/
  gamestravel
■ www.water-chariots.co.uk/
  gamestravel

London Travel Information
■ www.tfl.gov.uk
London Tourist Information
■ www.visitlondon.com
  Hotels, places to visit, events, travel and other important information.
Accessibility Information
■ www.london2012.com/
  accessibility
■ www.inclusivelondon.com

VISITORS' LONDON
ATLAS and GUIDE

© 2012 Copyright of the Publishers
Geographers' A-Z Map Company Limited
Fairfield Road, Borough Green, Sevenoaks, Kent TN15 8PP
Telephone: 01732 781000 (Enquiries and Trade Sales)
Telephone: 01732 783422 (Retail Sales)

An A-Z Publication   www.az.co.uk   Edition 35

PLACES OF INTEREST, MUSEUMS and ART GALLERIES in CENTRAL LONDON

Note 1. Each place name is followed by the reference to its map position; e.g. **Admiralty** Whitehall is to be found in square 4A on page 82. (Places preceded by an *asterisk are outside Central London area mapped.)

Note 2. Each station name is followed by the reference/s (abbreviated) to the Underground Line/s (or outside the Underground network the Main Line Railway Station) serving it. For example, Goodge Street N. means that station is on the Underground Northern Line.

Abbreviations are: B=Bakerloo; Cen.=Central; Cir.=Circle; D.=District; DLR=Docklands Light Railway; H.=Hammersmith & City; J.=Jubilee; M.=Metropolitan; N.=Northern; O.=Overground; P.=Piccadilly; V.=Victoria.

For central area Underground Map, see back cover.

RECOMMENDED SIGHTSEEING

✪✪✪ Places not to be missed ✪
✪✪ Highly recommended
✪ Recommended
✪ Recommended for families with children

■ *ACCESS FOR THE DISABLED*
Artsline, the online disability access information service, can provide up-to-date advice and access details to London's Museums, Galleries, Cinemas, Theatres, Concert Halls and other tourist attractions. 020 7388 2227.
www.artsline.org.uk
www.inclusivelondon.com

■ ***Abbey Road Recording Studios,** NW1, off Grove End Road / Circus Road. 3A 58 ✪
The world famous recording studios and nearby that iconic 'Beetles Album' zebra crossing. *Station:* St. John's Wood. J

■ **Admiralty & Admiralty Arch,** Whitehall. 4A 82
Once the administrative and operational centre of the British Navy. The Old Admiralty building dates from 1722 a handsome screen by Adam being added c.1760.
The large triple archway of Admiralty Arch opens on to the Mall and the quiet of St. James's Park. State and Royal processions pass through it on their way between Buckingham Palace and Westminster Abbey and/or the Houses of Parliament. *Station:* Charing Cross. B.N.

■ **Albert Memorial,** Kensington Gardens. 1E 89 ✪
Designed by Sir Gilbert Scott, it was erected as a memorial to Prince Albert, Consort of Queen Victoria, at a cost of £120,000, and took 20 years to construct.

Station: South Kensington. Cir.D.P.

■ **Alexander Fleming Museum,** St Mary's Hospital, Praed Street. 4A 66   The laboratory in which Fleming discovered penicillin, displays and video presentation. Admission charge. Open: 10 a.m. to 1 p.m. Mon. to Thurs. other times by appointment. *Station:* Paddington. B.Cir.D.H

■ **Apsley House,** Hyde Park Corner. 5A 80   ✪
This Adam's building was bought by the famous Duke of Wellington as his London House. It is now the Wellington Museum and contains trophies of the Napoleonic Wars, uniforms, swords and decorations.
Admission Charge. Open: Wed to Sun. 11 a.m. to 5 p.m. to 4pm winter. Closed: Mon. and Tues., Christmas and 1st January. *Station:* Hyde Park Corner. P.

■ **Bank of England,** Threadneedle Street. 5F 73
Known as the 'Old Lady of Threadneedle Street' this is the Governments Bank, incorporated under Royal Charter in 1694 to find for the Government £1,200,000 required for the war against France's Louis XIV. Only the massive external wall survives of Sir John Soanes' design of 1833.
Station: Bank. Cen. DLR. N.

■ **Bank of England Museum,** Bartholomew Lane. 4F 73
The history of the Bank of England from its foundation in 1694 to its role today as the nation's central bank. Displays include banknotes, coins, gold bullion, interactive videos and a reconstructed 18th century banking hall.
Open: Mon. to Fri. 10 a.m. to 5 p.m. Closed Sat. Sun. and Public Holidays. *Station:* Bank. Cen. DLR. N.

■ **Bankside Gallery,** Hopton Street. 2C 84
Gallery of the Royal Watercolour Society and Royal Society of Painter-Printmakers. Open during exhibitions daily 11 a.m. to 6 p.m. *Stations:* Blackfriars. Cir.D. Southwark. J.

■ **Banqueting House,** Whitehall 4B 82   ✪✪
Commissioned by James I, and built by Inigo Jones it was completed in 1622; and embellished by Charles I, with the famous painted ceiling by Rubens. The artist was rewarded with £3,000 and a knighthood. It was through a window of the Banqueting House that King Charles went to his execution in 1649. It is the only surviving building of Whitehall Palace. *Admission Charge.* Open: 10 a.m. to 5 p.m. Closed: Sundays, Bank Holidays, also 24 December to 1st January. Subject to closure during official functions. *Stations:* Charing Cross. B.N. Westminster. Cir.D.J.

■ **Barbican.** 2E 73 ✪ A large area of post-war redevelopment designed to reintroduce a balanced residential and cultural life back into the heart of the business City. Pedestrians are segregated from traffic on

3

elevated levels, and accommodation is grouped around squares, gardens and lakes. The historic church of St. Giles and a length of the Roman and Medieval City Wall are incorporated. The precinct includes the following: Barbican Centre for Arts and Conferences, Museum of London, Guildhall School of Music and Drama, City of London School for Girls.

Opened in 1982 the **Barbican Arts Centre** facilities include: Barbican Hall, Barbican Theatre, Barbican Library, Art Gallery, Cinemas, conference and trade exhibition space and roof-top Conservatory. Foyer open daily with exhibitions, bookshop and restaurants. Car park. *Stations:* Barbican. Cir.M.H. Moorgate. Cir.M.H.

■ **BBC Broadcasting House,** Portland Place. 3C 68
This famous landmark art deco building was completed in 1932, It houses the headquarters, sound division and new state-of-the-art multimedia centre of the British Broadcasting Corporation. *Station:* Oxford Circus. B.Cen.V.

■ **Belfast H.M.S.,** Morgan's Lane. 3C 86 🟢 🟢
This 10,500 ton cruiser, launched in 1938, the last major warship of the 1939-45 war still afloat, is now a naval museum and part of the Imperial War Museum.
Admission Charge. Open: Summer 10 a.m. to 6 p.m., Winter 10 a.m. to 5 p.m. Closed Christmas Eve and Day Boxing Day. *Station:* London Bridge. J.N.

■ **Benjamin Franklin House,** 36 Craven Street. 3B 82
18th century home of the American scientist, philosopher, printer, writer, inventor, diplomat and Founding Father of the United States, restored to its original period condition.
Admission Charge. Open for Historical Experience shows 12am. to 4.15pm. Wed. to Sun. Guided tours on Mondays. Pre book 020 7839 2006. *Stations:* Charing Cross. B.N. Embankment. Cir.D.

■ **Big Ben.** Westminster. 1C 94 🟢🟢🟢
Although popularly used to describe the clock tower, Big Ben is in fact the name of the 13$^{1}/_{2}$ ton bell which strikes the hours. It was cast at the Whitechapel Foundry in 1858. The tower stands 320 feet. *Station:* Westminster. Cir.D.J.

■ **Billingsgate,** Lower Thames Street. 2B 86
The name of London's oldest market, it was restricted in the 17th century to dealing in fish. The 1874 Market Hall facade is incorporated into the redeveloped site following the removal of trading to the Isle of Dogs in 1982.
Stations: Monument. Cir.D. Tower Hill. Cir.D.

■ **Bond Street.** 1C 80 The upper end which runs into Oxford Street is New Bond Street, and the lower end which runs into Piccadilly is Old Bond Street. This expensive London shopping street ranks in world fame with the Rue

de la Paix in Paris, and New York's Fifth Avenue.
Stations: Bond Street. Cen.J. Green Park. J.P.V.

■ **Borough Market,** Bedale Street. 4F 85   This important
wholesale market has, since 1998, been supplemented by
an ever growing, popular, award winning fine food retail
market crammed with both Londoner and tourist foodies
alike. Open Thurs. Fri. & Sat.. *Station*: London Bridge. J.N.

■ **BFI Southbank,** Southbank. 3E 83   British Film Institute
venue for creative, archive and themed film seasons. Bars,
restaurants, shop. BFI Library has an extensive collection
of books, periodicals and historic archive materials. Open
daily. *Stations*: Embankment. B.Cir.D. Waterloo. B.J.N.

■ **British Library,** 96 Euston Road. 3A 62   ✪✪✪
The worlds leading resource for scholorship and research,
its new climate controlled building has 11 reading rooms,
seating for 1200 researchers and nearly 14 million volumes
stored in 4 levels of basements.   The public exhibition
rooms include The Treasures Gallery housing some 200 of
the most famous items including Lindisfarne Gospels,
Magna Carta, Anglo-Saxon Chronicle, Gutenburg Bible,
Shakespeare's First Folio, Nelson's log books, Scott's
Antarctic Journal.   *Admission.   Treasures Gallery and
Public areas, cafe, bookshop* open Mon, Wed, Thurs, Fri:
9.30 a.m. to 6 p.m.   Tues: to 8 p.m.   Sat. to 5 p.m. Sun. 11
a.m. to 5 p.m. (*Reading Rooms* open to ticket holders only
for research only). Closed Christmas, and New Year.
Station:King's Cross St. Pancras. Cir.D.M.N.P.V.

■ **British Museum,** Great Russell Street. 3A 70   ✪✪✪ ✪
Originally founded in 1753 from several private collections
this rapidly became the finest Museum in existence. Its
unrivalled collections are comprised in the Departments of
Coins and Medals, Egyptian Antiquities, Western Asiatic
Antiquities, Greek and Roman Antiquities, (including the
famous Elgin Marbles), British and Medieval Antiquities
Oriental Antiquities and Prints and Drawings
   The famous former Reading Room is now the centrepiece
of the restored inner courtyard, a spectacular covered
public square 'The Great Court' with restaurants, museum
shops, education facilities; giving access both through the
museum and between the surrounding galleries.
Open: 10 a.m. to 5.30 p.m. daily and extended opening on
Fridays. Closed Christmas the New Year Day.
Free lectures on certain days.
Stations: Russell Square. P. Tottenham Court Road. C.N.

■ **Buckingham Palace,** The Mall, 1C 92   ✪✪✪
London Palace of Her Majesty Queen Elizabeth II. When
she is in residence the Royal Standard flies from the mast,
at other times the Union Flag is flown. Changing of the

Guard takes place daily at 11.30 a.m. on certain days, see *Pageantry* for details. Built by the Duke of Buckingham in 1703. Buckingham Palace was bought by George III in 1761, was rebuilt again by George IV, and became Queen Victoria's London home. Refaced in 1913. The Queen's Gallery, which forms part of the private chapel destroyed in the Second World War, contains a varying exhibition of masterpieces and works of art from the royal art treasures.

STATE ROOMS Open: During August and September by timed ticket only, Day tickets from Visitor Entrance ticket office. For details and advanced tickets Tel: 020 7766 7300 / 7301 or 7302. Admission Charge.

QUEEN'S GALLERY Open (except during changes of exhibition) 10 to 5.30pm daily. Admission by timed ticket, Tel: 020 7766 7301 for advance tickets. Admission charge.

ROYAL MEWS Open: Open 1 April - 31 October daily. Monday to Saturday at other times. Closed on specific days and State Visits; details and advanced tickets on Tel: 020 766 7302 Admission Charge. *Stations:* Green Park. J.P.V.

St. James's Park. Cir.D. Victoria. Cir.D.V.

■ ***Camden Lock Market,** Camden High Street, off Parkway 1B 60   A popular lively street market on Sat. and Sun. in an interesting canalside setting; clothes, crafts, antiques etc. *Station:* Camden Town. N.

■ ***Camden Passage,** N1   *Station:* Angel N.
A popular centre for antique arcades and shops.
Station: Angel. N.

■ ***Carlyle's House,** 24 Cheyne Row, SW3
The famous writer lived here from 1834 until his death in 1881. The house has hardly been altered since. Now a National Trust property. *Admission Charge.* Open: April to October 11 a.m. to 5p.m. Sat & Sun. 2pm to 5pm Wed. to Friday. *Station:* Sloane Square. Cir.D.

■ **Carnaby Street.** 5D 69
Popular teenage fashion centre of the late 1960's.
Stations: Oxford Circus. B. Cen. V. Piccadilly Circus. B.P.

■ **Cartoon Museum,** 35 Little Russell Street, 3B 70
See the finest examples of British cartoons, caricature and comic art from the 18th century to the present day. Resource centre and shop.
Admission Charge. Open: 10.30am to 5.30pm Tues. to Sat. 12.00 to 5.30 Sunday.
Station: Tottenham Court Road. Cen. N.

■ **Cenotaph, The,** Whitehall. 5B 82
Designed by Sir Edwin Lutyens, it now stands as a perpetual memorial to 'The Glorious Dead' of both World Wars. On the Sunday nearest November 11th of each year,

crowds gather at the Cenotaph for the two minutes silence, and wreaths are laid by the Queen, members of the Government and other mourners.
Stations: Charing Cross. B.N. Westminster. Cir.D.J.

Central Criminal Court, Old Bailey. 4B 72
Known as 'The Old Bailey', the present building was completed in 1907 on the site of Newgate Prison. The lofty tower is surmounted by a bronze gilt figure of Justice. During important trials in Court 1, a large crowd gathers outside in the hope of gaining admission to the Public Gallery in Newgate Street, which seats 28. Five other courts seat up to 32 each.
Open: 10.30-1pm, 2- 5pm (approx.) Monday to Friday. No children under 14 admitted. *Station:* St. Paul's. Cen.

Central Hall, Tothill Street 1A 94
This large domed building is the Methodists' London Headquarters. It is often used for conferences, exhibitions and concerts. The first session of the General Assembly of the United Nations took place here in 1946.
Stations: Westminster. Cir.D.J. St. James's Park. Cir.D.

Charles Dickens Museum 48 Doughty Street. 1E 7
Although the author lived here only from 1837 to 1839, 'Oliver Twist' and 'Nicholas Nickelby' were written and the 'Pickwick Papers' completed during those two years. The house is now a Museum of Dickens Memorabilia, and the headquarters of the Dickens Fellowship. *Admission Charge.* Open: 10a.m. to 5p.m. daily. (Closed April - Dec. 2012). Closed Bank Holidays. *Station:* Russell Square. P.

*Chelsea Physic Garden, 66 Royal Hospital Road, off Lower Sloane Street. SW3 5F 91.
Botanic gardens established in 1673 for the propagation and study of new species, from which several staple industries in former British colonies were derived. *Admission Charge.* Open: April to October Wed, Thurs, and Friday 12 to 5pm, Sunday and Bank Holidays 12 to 6pm. Entrance in Swan Walk, SW3.
Station: Sloane Square. Cir.D.

Cheshire Cheese, Ye Olde. Wine Office Court, 145 Fleet Street. 4A 72
An old and little-altered inn, famous for its Pudding, served at lunch times between Oct. and April. Tradition has it that Dr. Johnson Boswell and Oliver Goldsmith were habitues. Built in 1667 over cellars dating back to 1538.
Open: Bar daily Mon. to Sat. Restaurant Lunch daily, Dinner Mon. to Sat. *Station:* Blackfriars. Cir.D.

Chinatown. 1A 82
A lively centre of oriental sights, sounds and aromas, complete with chinese style gateways and telephone

boxes. Between Shaftesbury Avenue and Leicester Square. *Station:* Leicester Square. N. P.

■ **Christie's,** 8 King Street. 3E 81
Founded in 1766, greatly reputed for its auction sales of valuable paintings furniture, silver, jewels, etc. held regularly. Telephone 020 7839 9060 for details.
Station: Green Park. J.P.V.

■ **Churchill War Rooms,** King Charles Street. 5A 82 ✪✪
Used by Winston Churchill and his staff during World War II. Visit the cabinet room, central map room, Churchill's office and bedroom, the dining room, the transatlantic telephone room etc,. all restored to their wartime appearance. The Churchill Museum illustrates his life, work and achievements. *Admission charge.* Open 9.30 a.m. to 6 p.m. daily. Closed 24, 25 and 26 December.
Station: Westminster. Cir.D.J.

■ **City Hall,** Tooley Street. 4C 86
The unique spherical glass-walled headquarters of the Greater London Authority. Public access to landscaped piazzas and internal spiral ramp to the 10th floor viewing gallery with panoramic views. *Station:* London Bridge. J.N.

■ **Clarence House,** St. James's Palace. 5E 81 ✪✪
Built in the 1840's by designs by John Nash for the Duke of Clarence. A Royal residence for over 170 years but known primarily as the home of Queen Elizabeth the Queen Mother who lived here 1953-2002. Now official residence of the Prince of Wales. Open August and September 10 am to 4 pm. Admission by timed ticket only. Admission charge. 020 7766 7303 *Station:* Green Park. J.P.V.

■ **Cleopatra's Needle,** Victoria Embankment. 3D 83 ✪
An Egyptian obelisk which, about 3,500 years ago, stood in front of the Temple of the Sun at Heliopolis. When it was being towed to England in 1877, this 'Needle', 68½ feet high and weighing 180 tons, had to be abandoned in the Bay of Biscay during a storm. Its sister column is sited in Central Park, New York. *Station:* Embankment. B.Cir.D.N.

■ **Clink Exhibition,** The Clink Prison, 1 Clink Street. 3F 85
Illustrates the infamous low life of this area, once known as 'The Liberty of the Clink'. Admission Charge.
Open: Summer daily 10am to 9pm. Winter to 6 pm. Mon. to Fri., to 7.30 pm. Sat. and Sun. *Station:* London Bridge. J.N.

■ **Clock Museum,** see Guildhall.

■ **College of Arms,** or Heralds College, Queen Victoria Street. 1D 85   Deals with all matters relating to Heraldry genealogy and State Ceremonials and consists of three Kings of Arms (Garter, Clarenceux, and Norroy & Ulster),

six Heralds and four Pursuivants, appointed by the Sovereign. The building, Derby House, reconstructed after the Great Fire, was presented to the College by Queen Mary I (Mary Tudor) in 1554. The panelled Earl Marshal's Court is open 10 a.m. to 4 p.m. Mon. to Fri. (also open for heraldic enquiries). Closed public holidays.
Stations: Blackfriars. Cir.D. Mansion House. Cir. D.

County Hall, Westminster Bridge. 5D 75
Until 1986 the home of the Greater London Council (G.L.C.), now of the London Eye, London Sea Life Aquarium, restaurants, hotels and other leisure facilities.
Stations: Waterloo. B.J.N., Westminster. Cir.D.J.

Court Dress Collection, see Kensington Palace.

Courtauld Gallery, Somerset House. 1D 83 🟢🟢
Contains a famous collection of Impressionist and Post-Impressionist masterpieces by Matisse, Derain, Manet, Renoir, Van Gogh and Cezanne, and important works from the Renaissance through to the 20th century. Part of the Courtauld Institute of Art. See also Somerset House.
Admission Charge. Daily 10 a.m. to 6 p.m. Closed Christmas. *Stations:* Temple. Cir.D. Charing Cross. N.B.

Covent Garden, Southampton Street, WC2 1C 82 🟢🟢🟢
Originally 'Convent Garden' the square is now pedestrianised with the central market hall restored and open as an environment of shops, studios, cafes; promenades and paved areas are venues for lively street theatre. The Flower Market now houses the London Transport Museum.
The market given Royal Charter in 1671 grew into London's largest wholesale fruit, vegetable and flower market and has moved to a new site off Nine Elms Lane.
Stations: Covent Garden. P. Leicester Square. N. P.

Crafts Centre, Institute of Contemporary Applied Arts, 2 Percy Street, 3F 69   Federation of British Craft Societies mount fine exhibitions of work by artist-craftsmen. Open 10 a.m. to 6 p.m. Mon. to Sat.
Station: Tottenham Court Road. Cen. N.

Custom House, Lower Thames Street. 2B 86
Until 1940, the headquarters of the Commissioners of Customs and Excise, this has been the approximate site of successive Custom Houses from the 14th century. The impressive riverside facade is by Robert Smirke c.1825.
Stations: Monument. Cir.D. Tower Hill. Cir.D.

Cutty Sark, see Outer London. 🟢🟢🟢 🟢

Design Museum, Shad Thames. 5E 87
Covers the history, practice, theory and future of design in mass-produced consumer products and services.

Admission Charge. Open: 10 a.m. to 5.15 p.m. daily. *Stations:* London Bridge. J.N. Tower Hill. Cir.D. Tower Gateway. DLR.

- **Diana, Princess of Wales Memorial Fountain,** Hyde Park. 4A 78 Memorial to the late Princess who died 1997. *Stations:* Knightsbridge. P. Lancaster Gate. C.

- **Doctor Johnson's House,** 17 Gough Square. 4A 72
The famous 18th-century writer immortalised by Boswell, lived here from 1748 to 1759. The house contains an early edition of his Dictionary which was compiled here and published in 1755 selling for four guineas. Here also he wrote 'The Rambler' which appeared twice weekly for two years with a circulation of about five hundred.
Admission Charge. Open: 11 a.m. to 5.30 p.m. (Winter 5 p.m.). Closed Sundays and Bank Holidays.
Station: Chancery Lane. Cen.

- **Downing Street,** Whitehall. 5B 82 ☻
No.10 Downing Street is world-famous as the home of the British Prime Minister and the scene of Cabinet meetings. No. 11 houses the Chancellor of the Exchequer, and No. 12 is the Government Whip's office.
Station: Westminster. Cir.D.J.

- **Duke of York's Column,** Waterloo Place. 4F 81 ☻
This column, which stands above the steps leading to St. James's Park, is 124 feet high, and was erected in 1833 as a memorial to Frederick, Duke of York, the second son of George III. Although an able and devoted Army administrator, as Commander-in-Chief he was less successful in the field: according to popular song he 'led his ten thousand men up a hill and then he led them down again'! *Stations:* Piccadilly Circus. B.P. Charing Cross. B.N

- ***Earl's Court,** Warwick Road, SW5
Large exhibition halls for national events and important shows. *Stations:* Earls Court. D.P. West Kensington. D.

- **Ely Place.** 3A 72
The site of Ely Palace, London home of the Bishops of Ely in which John of Gaunt died in 1399. Demolished in 1772 it is now a private cul-de-sac of 18th century houses still watched over by a beadle at the gated entrance. The only remains are Ely Chapel or St. Etheldreda's Church the first pre-Reformation Church to be restored to Roman Catholic worship. *Station:* Farringdon. Cir.M.

- **Embankment Galleries,** Somerset House. 1E 83
Venue for themed exhibitions. See also **Somerset House.**
Admission Charge. Open: 10am. to 6 pm.

- **Eros,** see Piccadilly Circus. ☻☻☻

- **Faraday Museum** see Royal Institution Museum.

■ **Fashion Museum,** 83 Bermondsey Street. 5C 86
The first museum in the UK devoted to contemporary fashion and textiles. *Admission Charge.* Open 11 am to 6 pm. Tuesday to Saturday during exhibitions.
Station: London Bridge. J. N.

■ **Fleet Street,** 5F 71
Traditionally, but no longer the centre of the British newspaper industry, following the introduction of modern technology in new premises mainly on redeveloped dockland sites. *Stations:* Temple. Cir.D. Blackfriars. Cir.D.

■ **Florence Nightingale Museum,** Lambeth Palace Road, 1D 95   Illustrates the life and work of this famous woman, including a life size reconstruction of a ward at the Crimea. *Admission Charge.* Open: 10 a.m. to 5 p.m. daily. Closed Easter and Christmas.
Stations: Westminster. Cir.D.J. Waterloo. B.J.N.

■ **Foundling Museum,** 40 Bruswick Square. 5C 62
Interiors from the former Foundling Hospital, founded 1739 for the care of destitute children. Displays include pictures donated by Hogarth, Gainsborough, Knellar, also Handel's own copy of the 'Messiah'.
Admission Charge. Open 10 am. to 5 pm. Tues. to Sat., 11 to 5 pm. Sunday. *Station:* Russell Square. P.

■ **Garden Museum,** Lambeth Palace Road. 3D 95.
Permanant and temporary displays exploring themes on garden history, including chronology, tools and plant hunters - like the Tradescants - gardeners to Charles I, responsible for introducing many exotic plants into England; also related art exhibitions. *Admission charge.* Open: 10.30 am. to 5 pm. Sat. and Sun. to 4pm. Closed first monday of every month. *Station:* Westminster. Cir.D.J.

■ ***Geffrye Museum,** Kingsland Road, E2.
Housed in Almshouses erected in 1915 by the Ironmongers' Company. It comprises a series of period rooms dating from the 16th to the 20th century, containing furniture, domestic equipment and musical instruments from middle class homes. Open: 10 a.m. to 5 p.m. Sunday 12 to 5 p.m. Closed Mondays. (except Bank Holiday Mon). and Christmas. *Station:* Old Street. N.

■ **Globe Theatre,** see Shakespeare's Globe Theatre

■ **Golden Hinde,** St Mary Overie Dock, Cathedral Street. 3F 85 ✪ Floating museum ship, a full scale, ocean-going reconstruction of Sir Francis Drake's famous galleon. *Admission Charge.* Open: Daily 10 am to 5.30 pm unless closed for functions. *Station:* London Bridge. J.N.

■ **Goldsmiths' Hall,** Foster Lane. 4D 73
Home of the Goldsmiths' Company, one of the twelve

Great Livery Companies of the City of London. Since 1281 a jury containing several goldsmiths has been responsible for the Trial of the Pyx, the testing of newly minted coins, and from 1870 this has been held annually at Goldsmiths Hall. Gold and silver are assayed and hallmarked here, but the Assay Office is not open to the public.
Station: St. Paul's. Cen.

■ **Grant Museum of Zoology,** 21 University Street, 1F 69
Founded in 1828 as a teaching collection, its displays cover the whole Animal Kingdom, including many species now endangered or extinct. Open 1 to 5 p.m. Mon. to Fri.
Stations: Euston Square. Cir.D.H.

■ **Gray's Inn,** High Holborn. 2E 71 ✪
One of the four great Inns of Court. The historic Elizabethan Hall has been fully restored since the war. The Chapel also suffered damage by bombing. Francis Bacon, who was a student of the Inn, is said to have planted the catalpa tree in the gardens. *Station:* Chancery Lane. Cen. Holborn. Cen. P.

■ **Green Park.** 4C 80 ✪
Covers an area of 53 acres. The fine iron gateway on the Piccadilly side is that of old Devonshire House.
Stations: Green Park. J.P.V. Hyde Park Corner. P.

■ **Greenwich,** see Outer London. ✪✪✪ ✪

■ **Guard's Chapel,** see Guards Museum.

■ **Guards Museum,** Birdcage Walk. 1E 93
Illustrates the 300-year history of the Brigade of Guards. Adjacent is Guard's Chapel, rebuilt 1963 incorporating surviving apse of the earlier chapel devastated 1944 by a flying bomb during a morning service with the loss of 121 lives. *Admission Charge.* Open 10 a.m. to 4 p.m. daily
Station: St James's Park. Cir.D.

■ **Guildhall,** Gresham Street. 4F 73 ✪
The centre of civic government in the City of London for more than a thousand years. Dating from 1411-39 the structure of the present Hall survived both the Great Fire of 1666, and World War II bombs, though the only original interior is the fine medieval fan vaulted crypt.
The Great Hall is used for the Presentation of the Freedom of the City and other civic functions. Here the Livery Companies, twelve of whose banners hang from the walls, annually elect the new Lord Mayor and Sheriffs. The Lord Mayor's procession is held on the second Saturday in November and the banquet the following Monday.
A modern extension contains the **Guildhall Library,** a major public reference library specialising in the history of London, especially the City, it incorporates the **Clockmakers' Company Museum**—constituting the oldest

collection specifically of clock, watches and sundials in existance.

The **Guildhall Art Gallery** features both the collection of the Corporation of London—particularly rich in Victorian Art and the dramatically presented remains of the **Roman Ampitheatre** are preserved within the modern building.

Open: Guildhall (Subject to functions), 10 am to 4.30 pm daily, closed winter Sundays.
Library 9.30 am to 5 pm. Mon. to Sat. only.
Clock Museum 9.30 am to 4.45 pm Mon. to Sat. only.
Gallery and Ampitheatre 10am. to 5 pm. Mon. to Sat. 12.00 to 4pm. Sun. *Admission charge to special exhibitions.*
Station: Bank. Cen. DLR. N.

■ **Hampton Court Palace,** see Outer London ✪✪✪

■ **Handel House Museum,** 25 Brook Street. 1B 80
Handel's home from 1723 to his death 1759 and where he composed many famous works including Messiah and Music for the Royal Fireworks.
Note: entry is via Lancashire Court. *Admission charge.*
Open 10am to 6pm Tues to Sat, to 8pm Thurs. 12 to 6pm Sun. Closed Mondays. *Station:* Bond Street. Cen.J.

■ **Hatton Garden,** Holborn. 2A 72
Stands partly on the site of the old palace of the Bishop of Ely. It is well known as an important centre of the world's diamond trade. *Station:* Farringdon. Cir.H.M.

■ **Hayward Gallery,** Belvedere Road, South Bank. 4E 83 ✪
Changing shows of either modern art, a historical theme or international loan exhibitions. *Admission Charge.* Open 10 a.m. to 6 p.m. daily, to 10pm Fri. during exhibitions.
Stations: Embankment. B.Cir.D. Waterloo. B.J.N.

■ **H.M.S. Belfast.** See "Belfast". ✪✪ ✪

■ **Horse Guards,** Whitehall. 4B 82 ✪✪✪ ✪
These barracks were rebuilt in 1753. Two mounted guardsmen are on sentry duty here, and the Changing of the Guard daily at 11 a.m., Sundays 10 a.m., is a picturesque sight. Trooping the Colour, a magnificent ceremony, takes place on the Queen's official birthday on the parade ground at the rear of the building.
Stations: Charing Cross. B.N. Westminster. Cir.D.J.

■ **Household Cavalry Museum,** Horse Guards. 4B 82
Illustrates over 300 years of the colourful history of the Sovereign's mounted bodyguard. Formed 1661 the Household Cavalry consists of the two most senior regiments of the British Army, The Life Guards and Royal Horse Guards (The Blues). *Admission Charge.*
Open: Daily 10 a.m. to 6 p.m. Winter 5pm. Closed Christmas and Good Friday. *Stations:* Charing Cross. B.N. Westminster. Cir.D.J.

■ **Houses of Parliament,** Parliament Square. 1C 94 ✪✪✪
Stand throughout the world as a symbol of democratic
government. Rebuilt in 1840 on the site of the Old Palace
of Westminster, which was destroyed by fire, this is the
largest building erected in England since the Reformation.
When Parliament sits, a flag flies from Victoria Tower by
day, and by night a light shines high in the famous 'Big
Ben' clock tower. To hear debates during Parliamentary
sittings, queue at the Cromwell Gardens visitor entrance;
UK residents may obtain advance tickets from their MP.
Pre booked tours every Saturday and also during the
summer. Tours normally run most days except Sunday
between August and September. Tours are by timed ticket
only from ticket office, or in advance by telephone 0844
847 1672. *Station:* Westminster. Cir.D.J.

■ **Huntarian Museum,** Royal College of Surgeons, 35-43
Lincoln's Inn Fields. 5E 71 Contains the oldest medical
collection in the world and aims to encourage exploration
of the scientific, cultural and historical importance of the
museum collections. Open: 10 a.m. to 5 p.m. Tues. to Sat.
Station: Holborn. C. P.

■ **Hyde Park.** 3B 78 ✪✪
This Royal Park covers 341 acres, and together with
Kensington Gardens forms an oasis of green tranquillity.
Features near Hyde Park Corner include The Holocaust
Memorial Garden and Rose Garden, near Marble Arch is
Speaker's Corner famous for its Sunday 'tub thumping'
public orators. The Serpentine lake has pleasure boats for
hire and the lido is open for swimming in Summer months.
The Diana, Princess of Wales Memorial Fountain is
located near the Serpentine Bridge. Horse riding takes
place on Rotten Row. *Stations:* Hyde Park Corner. P.
Knightsbridge. P. Lancaster Gate. Cen. Marble Arch. Cen.

■ **Imperial War Museum,** Lambeth Road. 3A 96 ✪✪✪ ✪
Records and illustrates all aspects of warfare, military and
civil, allied and enemy, in which Britain and the
Commonwealth have been involved since August 1914.
Besides the machinery of war there are photographic and
film records, printed materials, also dramatic recreations
including 'Trench Experience' and 'Blitz Experience' with
sounds, smells and special effects. The Holocaust
Exhibition uses historical artifacts and poignant displays to
explain the persecution of the Jews and other groups
before and during World War II.
Open: 10 a.m. to 6 p.m. daily. Closed 24,25,26 December.
Stations: Lambeth North. B. Elephant and Castle. B.N.

■ **Jewish Museum,** 129/131 Albert Street. 1C 60
Illustrates British Jewish history, culture and faith; from

silver, ivory, wood and textile antiquities to a complete recreation of an East End Jewish street.
Admission Charge. Open: 10 a.m. to 5 p.m. Sunday to Thursday. 10 am to 2 pm. Friday. Closed Saturday. Bank Hols. & Jewish Festivals. *Station:* Mornington Crescent. N.

■ **Kensington Gardens.** 3D 77 ✪✪
Formerly the grounds of Kensington Palace, now a woodland park where children gather at the Round Pond to sail their boats, visit the statue of Peter Pan and explore the Diana, Princess of Wales Memorial Playground – the 7 mile long memorial walkway passes nearby. The Long Water should be seen from the bridge that divides it from the Serpentine. The Serpentine Gallery has changing and challenging exhibitions of modern art. *Stations:* High Street Kensington. Cir.D. Lancaster Gate. Cen. Queensway. Cen.

■ **Kensington Palace,** Kensington Gardens. 4C 76 ✪✪
Designed by Wren for William III, Queen Victoria was born here, was the home of Diana, Princess of Wales. The Palace's interiors have been restored to reflect their former grandeur. Within the State Apartments exhibitions include Victoria Revealed - focusing on Queen Victoria's Diamond Jubilee, also a special exhibition of some of Diana's dresses. *Admission Charge.* Open: Daily 10 am to 6 p.m. Summer. 10 a.m. to 5 p.m. Winter. Closed 24 - 26th December.
Stations: High Street Kensington. Cir.D. Queensway. Cen.

■ **Kew Gardens,** see Outer London. ✪✪

■ **Knightsbridge.** 1D 91 ✪
Famous area for high quality shopping, especially Harrods and Harvey Nichols. *Station:* Knightsbridge. P.

■ **Lambeth Palace,** Lambeth Palace Road. 3D 95
Has been for over 700 years the London residence of the Archbishop of Canterbury. Of particular interest is the historic public library founded in 1610 and freely open for research on application.
Stations: Westminster Cir.D.J., Lambeth North. B.

■ **Lancaster House,** Stable Yard Road. 5D 81
This early Victorian mansion is known for the splendour of its State Apartments.*Stations:* Green Park. J.P.V., St. James's Park. Cir.D.

■ **Leadenhall Market,** Leadenhall Street. 5B 74
Victorian glass and Iron hall of 1881. Once specialised in poultry, now in quality delicatessen shops.
Station: Monument. Cir.D.

■ **Leicester Square.** 2A 82 ✪
Was laid out from 1635-70, and named after the Earl of Leicester, whose residence was on its north side. Hogarth

and Joshua Reynolds also lived here.
Station: Leicester Square. N.P.

■ ***Leighton House Museum,** 12 Holland Park Road, W14
Home and studio of the Victorian artist Frederic, Lord
Leighton 1830-96, features include an amazing Arab Hall
decorated with 13th-17th c. middle eastern tiles.
Admission charge. Open daily except closed Tuesdays.
Closed Christmas Jan 1st.

■ **Lincoln's Inn,** Chancery Lane. 4E 71 ✪
One of the four inns of Court which have the power of
'calling to the Bar'. The Law Library, built in 1845, is the
finest in London and contains over 70,000 volumes and
many fine MSS. Of particular interest are the early 16th
century gateway to Chancery Lane and the Inigo Jones
chapel consecrated in 1623.
Admission: To the Inn and Library on appointment. To the
Chapel, free Sunday service 11.30 a.m., during sittings.
Stations: Chancery Lane. Cen. Holborn. Cen.P.

■ **Lloyd's,** Lime Street. 5B 74
This international insurance market and world centre of
shipping intelligence is named after Edward Lloyd's coffee
house, the 17th-century rendezvous of people interested in
shipping. The famous Lutine Bell is rung when an
announcement of special importance is to be made from
the Rostrum, particularly with regard to overdue vessels.
The exciting modern building has external observation lifts
and service ducting in strong colours; the whole building
being well and dramatically illuminated at night.
Stations: Aldgate. Cir.N. Bank. Cen.N. Monument. Cir.D

■ **Lombard Street.** 5A 74
Famous as the centre of banking, it owes its name to the
Jewish Lombard goldsmiths and money-lenders who
established themselves here after their expulsion in 1290.
Station: Bank. Cen.DLR.N.

■ **London Bridge.** 3A 86
There have been many bridges on this site, the first having
been built by the Romans. The present bridge replaced
the 1831 stone bridge, now in Lake Havasu City, Arizona
U.S.A. *Stations:* London Bridge. J.N. Monument. Cir.D.

■ **London Bridge Experience,** Tooley Street. 3A 86 ✪ ✪
An exploration of the history of London Bridge from Roman
and Medieval times combining special effects and
entertaining displays.
Admission Charge. Open Mon. to Fri. 10 am. to 5 pm. Sat.
& Sun. to 6 pm. *Station:* London Bridge. J.N.

■ **London Canal Museum,** New Wharf Road. IC 62
Tells the story of London's canals, including the role of

working horses; housed in what was an industrial ice house built in the 1850's for Carlo Gatti the ice cream manufacturer. *Admission Charge.*
Open: Tues. to Sun. and Bank Holiday Mondays 10 a.m. to 4.30 p.m. Closed on other Mondays.
Station: King's Cross St. Pancras. Cir.D.P.N.V.M.H.

■ **London Dungeon,** Tooley Street. 4A 86 ✪ ✪
An exhibition of gruesome and macabre events from the Dark Ages until the end of the 17th century, not recommended by the management to the nervous or unaccompanied children.   *Admission Charge.*
Open: Daily. *Station:* London Bridge. J.N.

■ **London Eye,** Old County Hall. 5D 83 ✪✪✪ ✪
The world's highest observation wheel provides spectacular views over London from one of 32 enclosed capsules. Gradual 30 minute ride reaches 450ft above the River Thames. An iconic landmark and a symbol of modern London. *Admmission charge.* Open daily. Closed Christmas Day and for end of January maintainace.
Stations: Westminster. Cir.D.J. Waterloo. B.J.N.

■ **London Film Museum,**
- Old County Hall. 5D 83 *Station:* Westminster. Cir.D.J.
- Russell Street, Covent Garden. 1C 82 *Station:* Covent Garden. P. Exhibitions illustrating the history of movie making, interactive displays, sets, costumes etc.
Admission charge. Open daily.

■ **London Pavilion,** see Piccadilly Circus.

■ **London's Death Trap,** Old County Hall. 5D 83
Audio visual pseudo horror experience. *Admission charge,*
Open daily. *Stations:* Westminster. Cir.D.J. Waterloo. B.J.N

■ **London Sea Life Aquarium,** Old County Hall. 5D 83
✪✪ ✪ One of Europe's largest exhibits of fish and marine life from around the world features huge Atlantic and Pacific Ocean tanks. Also many other displays including European and Exotic habitats, touch pools etc.
Admission Charge. Open Mon. to Thurs. 10 am. to 6 pm. Fri. to Sun. 10 am to 7 pm. *Station:* Westminster. Cir.D.J.

■ **London Stone,** Cannon Street. 1F 85
This stone is believed to have been the millarium from which the Romans measured the distances out of the City.
Station: Cannon Street. Cir.D.

■ **London Transport Museum,** Covent Garden. 1C 82
✪✪ ✪ Historic vehicles and exhibits including early steam and electric locomotives, horse-buses, motor buses (including the famous 'B' type), tram cars, trolley buses, posters, tickets, signs, etc. Sit in the driving seat of a

London Bus or Underground Train; historical films show London as it was. Housed in a magnificent Victorian structure with cast iron arcades and glazed clerestories. *Admission Charge.* Open 10 a.m. to 6 p.m. Saturday to Thursday. 11 am to 6 pm Friday. Closed Christmas Day and Boxing Day *Station:* Covent Garden. P.

■ **London Zoo,** Regent's Park. 1F 59 ✪✪✪✪
The 'lure of the wild' in the heart of London; with over 750 species of animal this is a day out with a difference.
Special attractions include Penguin Beach, Gorilla Kingdom, the walk through Tropical Jungle Bird Pavilion, Butterfly Paradise the Rainforest Lookout biome and Nightzone with its nocturnal animal displays. Animal Adventure, a childrens zoo experience allows children to immerse themselves in the sights, sounds and smells of life in the animal kingdom. Various animal encounters and animal feeding take place at certain times during the day. *Admission Charge.* Open daily. Closes earlier in Winter months. Closed only Christmas Day.
Stations: Camden Town. N. Regent's Park. B.

■ **Madame Tussaud's,** Marylebone Road. 1F 67 ✪✪✪✪
The world-famous waxwork exhibition and tourist attraction, where visitors wander among themed displays featuring life-like historical, showbiz and contemporary figures. *Admission charges vary.* Open daily. Closed only on Christmas Day. *Station:* Baker Street. B.Cir.J.M.H

■ **Mansion House.** 5F 73
Official home of the Lord Mayor of London, built in 1753 as one of London's grandest Georgian town palaces, the famous banquets given by the Lord Mayor take place in the Egyptian Hall. Tours of the magnificent interiors and historic treasures take place on Tuesdays 2pm. (closed August). *Admission charge. Station:* Bank. Cen. DLR.N.

■ **Marble Arch,** Oxford Street. 1E 79
Originally intended as an entrance to Buckingham Palace, this 'triumphal arch' was made too narrow for the State Coach and was utilised as a gate into Hyde Park. Later, the park boundary was moved back, leaving Marble Arch an entrance to nowhere. Nearby, where Edgware Road intersects Bayswater Road, stood Tyburn Gallows, where public executions took place until 1783.
Station: Marble Arch. Cen.

■ **Marlborough House,** Pall Mall. 4F 81
Built by Wren in 1709 for the Duke of Marlborough, it reverted to the Crown in 1817. Amongst its occupants have been Edward VII when Prince of Wales, and George V until his accession. From 1911 until her death it was the residence of Queen Alexandra. Queen Mary lived here

when in London. Now a Commonwealth Conference Centre.
Adjoining the house is QUEEN'S CHAPEL 1627, designed by Inigo Jones. Services: Sun 8.30 and 11.15 a.m. Easter Day—end of July.
Station: Green Park. J.P.V.

■ **MCC Cricket Tour & Museum,** Lord's Cricket Ground. 4A 58 Tours including entry to museum of cricket memorabilia and home of The Ashes. Regular tours daily, for advanced booking Tel 020 7616 8595. Restrictions apply on match days,
Admission Charge. *Station:* St. John's Wood. J.

■ **Monument, The.** 1A 86 ✪
A fluted Doric column erected by Sir Christopher Wren in the year 1677 to commemorate the Great Fire of London of 1666. Its height is 202 feet, which is the distance to the house in Pudding Lane where the fire broke out.
The magnificent view of the City from the top well repays the effort of ascending the 311 steps.
Admission Charge. Open daily 9.30 am to 5.30pm.
Station: Monument. Cir.D.

■ ***Museum of Brand's and Packaging,** 2 Colville Mews, Lonsdale Road, off Westbourne Grove 5A 64.
History of consumer culture and shopping habits through printed material, packaging and advertising.
Admission charge. Open Tues to Saturday 10am to 6pm. Sundays 11 to 5. *Station:* Notting Hill Gate. Cen.Cir.D.

■ **Museum of Childhood,** see Outer London.

■ **Museum of London,** London Wall. 3D 73 ✪ ✪
One of London's modern purpose-built museums: constructed as part of the Barbican. Imaginative displays include London before London; Roman London, Medieval London; Tudor & early Stuart London and Modern London, the story of London and its people from 1666 up to the present. See also Museum of London Docklands.
Open: Daily 10 a.m. to 6 p.m. Closed Christmas and Boxing Day. *Stations:* Barbican. Cir.M.H. St. Paul's. Cen

■ **Museum of Methodism,** see Wesley's House.

■ **Music Museum,** Royal Academy of Music, 1A 68
One of the finest collections of musical instruments maintained in playing condition, also archives, musical memorabilia and original manuscripts..
Open 11.30 to 5.30pm Mon. to Fri. 12 noon-4pm Saturdays. *Station:* Baker Street. B.Cir.J.M.H.

■ ***National Army Museum,** Royal Hospital Road, off Lower Sloane Street. SW3 5F 91. ✪ Museum of the British Army, and of the Indian Army to 1947 also colonial and

auxiliary forces.
Open: 10 a.m. to 5.30 p.m. daily. Closed Good Friday, Christmas Eve and Day, Boxing Day and New Year's Day. *Station:* Sloane Square. Cir.D.

■ **National Film Theatre,** see BFI Southbank.

■ **National Gallery,** Trafalgar Square. 2A 82 ✪✪✪
The Gallery was opened in 1824 with the Angerstein Collection of 38 pictures, it has developed into one of the most important picture galleries in the world, containing a collection representative of every European school of painting and works by nearly all the Great Masters.
In addition special exhibitions of great interest are mounted throughout the year.
Open: 10 a.m. to 6 p.m.; Friday to 9 p.m. Closed Christmas Eve and Day, Boxing Day and Good Friday. Free lectures on certain days. *Station:* Charing Cross. B.N.

■ **National Maritime Museum,** see Outer London. ✪✪✪✪

■ **National Portrait Gallery,** St. Martin's Place. 2A 82 ✪✪
National collection of painted and photographic portraits of famous British men and women dating mainly from the Tudor dynasty to the twentieth century. Special exhibitions throughout the year.
Open: 10 a.m. to 6 p.m. daily. Thurs. and Fri. to 9pm. Closed 24, 25 and 26th December. *Stations:* Leicester Square. N.P. Charing Cross. B.N.

■ **National Theatre,** see South Bank Arts Centre

■ **Natural History Museum,** Cromwell Rd. 3F 89 ✪✪✪✪
One of the world's finest natural history collections; organised into *Blue and Green Zones*- dinosaurs, insects, ecology, human biology, mammals, sea life, origin of species etc and *Red Zones*- ancient and future earth, changing landcapes including an Earthquake Experience. The new Darwin Centre enables visitors to see displays from the many millions of zoological specimens gathered by scientists for 400 years. Activity sheets available for children.   Open: 10 a.m. to 5.50 p.m. daily. Closed 24, 25, 26th December. *Station:* South Kensington. Cir.D.P.

■ **New Scotland Yard,** Broadway. 2F 93
The Headquarters of the Metropolitan Police and of its Criminal Investigation Department. Formerly situated on Victoria Embankment. Admission: visiting police officers only.   *Station:* St. James's Park. Cir. D.

■ **Old Operating Theatre Museum,** 9a St. Thomas' St. 4F 85 An original Victorian operating theatre and Herb Garret, with instruments and apparatus illustrating medical history, and the history of St. Thomas's and Guy's Hospitals.
Admission Charge. Open: 10.30 a.m. to 5 p.m. daily.

Station: London Bridge. J.N.

■ ***Olympia,** Hammersmith Road, W14.
It covers an area of 10¾ acres, and is one of the most famous showplaces and exhibition centres in the world.
Station: Kensington (Olympia). D. (Exhibitions only)

■ **Oratory, The,** Brompton Road. 3B 90 ✪
Built in the Italian Renaissance style during the 19th century, it is well known for its fine musical services. Cardinal Newman served here as priest after his conversion from the Anglican to the Roman Catholic faith.
Open: 6 a.m. to 8 p.m. *Station:* South Kensington. Cir.D.P.

■ **Oxford Street.** 5B 68 ✪
One of Londons principal shopping streets, famous for its many department stores including Selfridges, John Lewis, Debenhams. Remarkably straight for London, it is on the site of the old Roman road leading west from the city.
Stations: Bond Street. Cen.J. Marble Arch. Cen. Oxford Circus. B.Cen.V. Tottenham Court Road. Cen.N.

■ **Oxo Tower Wharf,** South Bank 2A 84 ✪
A South Bank landmark, this imposing wharf is now a showpiece centre for artist designer-craftsmen; rooftop restaurant and 8th floor public viewing gallery.
See also Gabriel's Wharf nearby.
Stations: Waterloo. B.J.N. Blackfriars.Cir.D. Southwark. J.

■ **Petrie Museum,** University College. 1F 69
Egyptian and Sudanese archaeology illustrating life in the Nile Valley from prehistory through to the time of the pharaohs, the Ptolemaic, Roman Coptic and Islamic periods. Open: Tues to Sat. 1 to 5 p.m. Closed Christmas and Easter holidays. *Station:* Euston Square. Cir. M. H.

■ **'Petticoat Lane',** Middlesex Street. 3D 75 ✪
A street market for a numerous variety of goods where on Sunday mornings, bargain-hunters and passers-by are attracted to the stalls of persuasive salesmen.
Stations: Aldgate East. D.M., Liverpool Street. Cen.Cir.M.

■ **Photographers Gallery,** 16-18 Ramillies Street, 5D 69
Changing exhibitions by the latest emerging talent, to historical archives and established artists. Talks, workshops and study room. Bookshop and print sales.
Station: Oxford Circus. B. Cen. V.

■ **Piccadilly Circus.** 2F 81 ✪✪✪
A swirl of people, traffic and coloured lights; this is the traditional focal point of London. A pedestrian piazza links the famous Eros statue to the south side; both the Trocadero Centre and the London Pavilion provide traffic free environments of shopping and leisure facilities.
Station: Piccadilly Circus. B.P.

■ **Pollocks Toy Museum,** 1 Scala Street. 3E 69 ✪
Of particular interest to children of all ages. Toy theatres,
games dolls, dolls' houses and toys, etc.
Admission Charge. Open: 10 a.m. to 5 p.m. Mon. to Sat.
Closed Sun.; Christmas and Boxing Days and Easter Mon.
Station: Goodge Street. N.

■ ***Portobello Road Market,** Portobello Road, off Pembridge
Road W11 2A 76. ✪
Famous for its Saturday market of antiques, Victoriana,
pseudo-antiques, but the rest of the week Portobello and
the surrounding streets are a lively mix of general market
stalls, exotic food shops, fashion shops and restaurants.
Station: Ladbroke Grove. M. Westbourne Park. M.

■ **Queen's Gallery,** see Buckingham Palace. ✪

■ **Queen Victoria Memorial,** The Mall. 5D 81 ✪
Stands in front of Buckingham Palace. Of white marble the
centre figure of the Queen is 13 ft high. Groups on the
remaining sides represent Justice, Truth and Motherhood
while the whole is surmounted by a winged Victory.
Stations: St. James's Park. Cir.D. Victoria. Cir.D.V. Green
Park. J.P.V.

■ **Raven Row Gallery,** 56 Artillery Lane. 3D 75
Changing exhibitions of challenging contemporary art
within an historic 18th c. Huguenot silk merchants shop.
Open: 11 am. to 6 pm. Wed. to Sun.
Station: Liverpool Street. Cen. Cir. M

■ **Regent's Park,** 2E 59 ✪✪
One of the largest London parks, this Royal Park covers an
area of 472 acres and contains the Zoo and a large
boating lake. Queen Mary's Gardens are famous for roses
and the open-air theatre The formal Italianate Avenue
Gardens contrast with the informal English Gardens.
The elegant and imposingly classical Regency terraces
surrounding the Park by John Nash are now well
contrasted by two modern buildings, the Royal College of
Physicians and the London Central Mosque.
Stations: Baker Street. B.Cir.J.M. Regent's Park. B.

■ **Regent Street.** 1D 81 ✪
This important shopping street was first designed by Nash
in 1813 as a link between Carlton House and Regent's
Park. It is now famous for its quality shops, fashion houses
and department stores like Liberty and the toy emporium
Hamleys.
Stations: Oxford Circus. B.Cen.V. Piccadilly Circus. B.P.

■ **Ripley's Believe IT or Not!** London Pavilion. 2F81
Collection of odd and bizarre objects from around the

world. *Admission Charge.* Open: 10 a.m. to 12 am. daily, *Station:* Piccadilly Circus. B.P

■ **Roman Amphitheatre,** see Guildhall

■ **Roosevelt Memorial,** Grosvenor Square. 1A 80
Britain's personal memorial to President Franklin D. Roosevelt after the Second World War. 160,000 contributions of five shillings each closed the subscription list in less than 6 days. *Station:* Bond Street. Cen.J.

■ **Rose Theatre,** 56 Park Street. 3E 85
Site of the first theatre on Bankside built 1587, and venue for Shakespeare plays before the opening of the nearby famous Globe Theatre. *Admission May to Sept. via tours pre booked though Shakespeare's Globe Theatre see below. Station:* London Bridge. J.N

■ **Royal Academy of Arts,** Burlington House, Piccadilly.
2E 81 ✪✪✪   Founded by George III in 1768 with Sir Joshua Reynolds as its first President and located at Somerset House, the Academy moved here to the town house of the Earls of Burlington 1869. Many varied special exhibitions of great interest are held throughout the year, while the famous annual Summer Exhibition is of works for sale and by living artists and is open to all. *Admission Charge.* Open: 10 a.m. to 6 p.m. daily, to 10.00 pm. Fri. *Stations:* Piccadilly Circus. B.P. Green Park. J.P.V.

■ **Royal Air Force Museum,** See Outer London. ✪✪✪ ✪

■ **Royal Albert Hall,** Kensington Gore. 1F 89 ✪
This largest Concert Hall in London, seating over 5,000 was completed in 1871. Home of the famous annual season of BBC Proms concerts.
Station: South Kensington. Cir. D.P.

■ **Royal Ceremonial Dress Collection,** see Kensington Palace

■ **Royal College of Music,** Prince Consort Road. 2F 89
The Royal College of Music museum of instruments contains an internationally renowned collection of over 800 instruments from c.1480 to present day. Here also is the acclaimed Britten Opera Theatre opened 1987. *Open:* in times, Tues to Fri. 11.30 am to 4.30 pm. and throughout the summer. *Station:* South Kensington. Cir.D.P.

■ **Royal College of Surgeons,** Lincoln's Inn Fields, 4E 71
Is the headquarters of surgery in England. Teaching, research and examinations are major functions of the College.   For Huntarian Museum see above. *Station:* Holborn. Cen.P.

■ **Royal Courts of Justice,** Strand, WC2. 5E 71
These buildings were opened in 1882, enlarged in 1911 and extended in 1968 and 1971. There are 50 Courts, and

visitors are admitted to the public galleries. Courts generally sit in Term times: Weekdays, 10.30 a.m. to 4.30 p.m. *Station:* Temple. Cir.D.

■ **Royal Exchange,** Cornhill. 5A 74
Opened by Queen Victoria in 1844, the previous two buildings on this site burned down respectively in 1666 and 1838. The original Exchange of 1568 was modelled on the Antwerp Bourse. *Station:* Bank. Cen.DLR.N.

■ **Royal Festival Hall,** see South Banks Arts Centre.

■ **Royal Geographical Society,** Kensington Gore. 1F 89
Founded in 1830. Lowther Lodge was designed by Norman Shaw 1874. Important cartographic library, bibliographic archives and expedition relics.
Changing exhibitions open 10 a.m. to 5 p.m. Mon. to Fri. Closed Sat. and Sun. Reading Room for study and research, fees may apply. *Station:* Knightsbridge. P

■ ***Royal Hospital, Chelsea,** Royal Hospital Road, off Lower Sloane Street, SW3. 5F 91 🟢
Was designed by Sir Christopher Wren and founded in 1682 by Charles II as a home for old soldiers. The 'Chelsea Pensioner' is a well-known figure in his scarlet (Summer) or dark blue (Winter) coat. The statue of Charles II in the Figure Court is by Grinling Gibbons. In part of the spacious gardens the Chelsea Flower Show is held annually by the Royal Horticultural Society.
Open: **Museum** 10am to 12pm and 2pm to 4pm Mon. to Fri. **Great Hall** 11am to 12pm and 2pm to 4pm. Mon. to Sat. **Chapel** 10am to 12pm and 2pm to 4 pm Mon. to Sat. **The grounds** are open from 10am to dusk.
Station: Sloane Square. Cir.D.

■ **Royal Institution Museum,** Albermarle Street. 2D 81
The home of world changing science since 1799, themed displays - experimentation, people and communication include Faradays 1850's magnetic laboratory and a current state-of-the-art nanotechnology museum.
Open Monday to Friday 9 am to 6 pm. *Stations:* Green Park. J.P.V. Piccadilly Circus. B.P.

■ **Royal Mews,** see Buckingham Palace. 🟢🟢 🟢

■ **Royal Mint,** Tower Hill, 2E 87
It was here that our 'silver' and bronze coins were struck between 1811 and 1970, work since transferred to Llantrisant, South Wales. Prior to 1811 it was located in the Tower of London. *Station:* Tower Hill. Cir.D.

■ **Royal Naval College,** see Outer London. 🟢

■ **Royal National Theatre,** see National Theatre.

■ **Royal Opera House,** Bow Street, 5C 70
The home of the Royal Opera and Royal Ballet

companies, now fully modernised and restored with public areas, exhibition spaces and restaurants.
Open Mon to Sat. *Station:* Covent Garden. P.

■ **Saatchi Gallery,** Duke of Yorks HQ, King's Road 5E 91
Besides changing exhibitions from the avant-garde Saatchi Collection of modern art, the Gallery aims to provide an innovative forum for contemporary art, presenting work by largely unseen young artists or by established international artists whose work has been rarely or never exhibited in the UK.
Open daily 10am to 6pm. *Station:* Sloane Square. Cir. D.

■ **St. Bartholomew's Hospital and Museum,** Smithfield.
3C 72 Popularly known as 'Bart's', this is the oldest hospital in London, having been founded in 1123 by Rahere, together with an Augustine Priory, in the reign of Henry I. Its long history, artifacts and historic medical instruments are displayed in the Museum. Also in the hospital are portraits of famous physicians and surgeons by Reynolds, Lawrence, etc., and Hogarth's 'The Good Samaritan and 'Pool of Bethesda'.
Admission charge: Open 10am. to 4 pm. Tues to Fri only. Closed Bank Hols. *Station:* St. Paul's. Cen.

■ **St. James's Palace.** 4E 81 ✪
Built in 1532 by Henry VIII on the site of a leper hospital, this Palace was from time to time used as a Royal Residence after the Palace of Whitehall had been burned down in 1698. Charles II, James II, Mary II and George IV were born here. It was from here that Charles I took leave of his children before walking across St. James's Park to his execution, outside the Banqueting House. The main gateway, the Tapestry and Armoury Rooms and the Chapel Royal are all that remain of the original building.
Admission: To the Chapel for the Sunday morning service at 8.30 and 11.15 October to Good Friday. See also Clarence House and Marlborough House.
Stations: Green Park. J.P.V., St. James's Park. Cir.D.

■ **St. James's Park.** 5F 81 ✪✪
These 93 acres were acquired by Henry VIII in 1531 to give him hunting near his Palace of Whitehall. It was under Charles II that the land was laid out by the French landscape gardener, Le Notre, to form one of the most charming of London's Royal Parks. A variety of water birds inhabit the lake, and these may be identified by labelled reproductions.
Stations: St. James's Park. Cir.D., Charing Cross. B.N

■ **St. Katharine Docks,** St. Katharine-by-the-Tower. 2E 87
✪ Built 1827 to designs by Thomas Telford, these massive and secure warehouses were used to store

25

valuable cargoes from all over the world. Historic structures have been restored and incorporated into a precinct of shopping arcades, restaurants and cobbled walks around a 240 moorings Yacht Haven.
Station: Tower Hill. Cir.D. Tower Gateway. DLR.

■ **St. Martin-in-the-Fields,** St. Martin's Place 2B 82 ✪
This historic church rebuilt by James Gibbs 1721-61 is famous as a landmark in Trafalgar Square, also for its work with the homeless and public concerts. Gift shop, Cafe in the Crypt and London Brass Rubbing Centre (see below)
Station: Charing Cross. B.N.

■ **St. Paul's Cathedral,** St Paul's Churchyard. 5C 72 ✪✪✪
This is Sir Christopher Wren's masterpiece, built to replace the much larger Medieval Cathedral on the same site after its destruction in the Great Fire of 1666. The most prominent of London's buildings, this is an immense Renaissance structure, its exterior length being 515 ft, its width across transepts 250 ft., and the height from pavement to the top of the cross 365 ft. Together with many other chapels in St. Paul's there is the American Chapel, which was dedicated in the presence of Queen Elizabeth II and the then Vice-President Nixon of the United States. Among the many famous people buried here are Christopher Wren, Nelson, Wellington, Jellicoe, Reynolds and Turner. 627 steps lead to the Whispering Gallery, Stone Gallery and to the Great Ball.
Services held daily.
Open for visitors Mon. to Sat. 8.30 a.m. to 4 p.m. *Admission Charge for sightseers.* Visiting subject to restrictions during services and ceremonies. Open on Sundays for services only. *Station:* St. Paul's. Cen.

■ **Savoy Chapel,** Savoy Hill, Strand. 1D 83
The Queen's Chapel of the Savoy belongs to Her Majesty The Queen and is a private chapel of the Sovereign in her right as Duke of Lancaster. It does not fall within any bishop's jurisdiction, but remaining firmly within the Church of England; it is also the Chapel of the Royal Victorian Order. The present Chapel was erected as part of a hospital founded under the will of Henry VII. It stands on the site of the old Palace of Savoy given to the Earl of Savoy by Henry III. Chaucer, it is believed, was married here during John of Gaunt's ownership. John of Gaunt had to flee, however when Wat Tyler's rebels destroyed the buildings in 1381. Open: Tues. to Fri. 11.30 a.m. to 3.30 p.m. Sun. service 11.00 a.m. Closed August and September. *Station:* Embankment. B.Cir.D.N.

■ **Science Museum,** Exhibition Road. 3F 89 ✪✪✪ ✪
Renowned collection arranged in themed displays to illustrate the history of science and technology,

development of engineering, transport and important industries. Among the great many iconic artifacts on display are the worlds first industrial steam engines, the locomotive 'Rocket', 'Penny-Farthing' cycle, Model T Ford motor car, the first trans-Atlantic aircraft, the experimental vertical take-off 'Flying Bedstead', Apollo 10 capsule. Other features include an IMAX cinema and many interactive galleries for children like Launch Pad,
Open: daily 10 a.m. to 6 p.m. Closed 24, 25, 26 December. *Station:* South Kensington. Cir.D.P.

Serpentine Gallery, Kensington Gardens. 4A 78
Serpentine Sackler Gallery, Magazine building 3A 78.
Changing and challenging exhibitions of modern art.
Open daily 10am to 6pm. during exhibitions.
Stations: South Kensington. Cir.D.P. Lancaster Gate. Cen

Shakespeare's Globe Theatre & Exhibition, Bankside
3D 85   ✪✪   This reconstructed 1599 Globe Theatre, is the first thatched building to be built in the centre of London since the Great Fire 1666. Theatre Tour and Exhibition devoted to Shakespeare and the London in which he worked and lived is open throughout the year, summer season of plays in the open air Globe Theatre.
Admission Charge. Open: Summer months; Globe Theatre tour & exhibition am daily, exhibition and Rose Theatre Tour pm daily. Winter months daily Globe Theatre tour & exhibition 10 am. to 5 pm. daily. Closed 24 and 25th December. Tel: 020 7902 1500.
Summer Season of plays - Box Office 020 7401 9919.
Stations: London Bridge. J.N. Southwark. J.

Sherlock Holmes Museum, 221b Baker Street. 1E 67
Modelled on the life and times of Sherlock Holmes and Dr Watson as portrayed by Sir Arthur Conan Doyle.
Admission Charge. Open 9.30 a.m. to 6 p.m. daily. Closed 25th Dec. *Station:* Baker Street. B.Cir.J.M.H.

Sikorsky Museum, 20 Princes Gate. 1A90. Collection of Polish Institute and Sikosky memorabilia. Open Tues. to Fri, 2pm to 4pm. *Station:* South Kensington. Cir.D.P.

Silver Vaults, 53 Chancery Lane. 3F 71
Undergound strongrooms built in the 1880s as a Safe Depository. Now houses over 40 individual shops selling all types of silverware from contemporary to antique and Sheffield Plate. *Station:* Chancery Lane. Cen.

Sir John Soane's Museum, Lincoln's Inn Fields. 3E 71 ✪
This house was designed and built in 1812 by Sir John Soane, architect to the Bank of England, to contain his own museum, furniture, and library. Among the many unique exhibits are Egyptian, Greek and Roman antiquities, including the Sarcophagus of Seti 1; paintings by

27

Canaletto, Watteau and Reynolds; and the finest collection of Hogarth's work, comprising the eight scenes of 'The Rake's Progress' and four of 'The Election'.
Open: Tuesday to Saturday, 10 a.m. to 5 p.m. Closed Mon. and Bank Holidays. *Station:* Holborn. Cen.P.

■ **Smithfield.** 3C 72
Now chiefly known for its Meat Market. In the past, the 'smooth field' lying outside the city wall was variously used for jousting, for St. Bartholomew's Fair (held annually for centuries), and for many executions. Among those executed here were: William Wallace, beheaded in 1305 for supporting Robert Bruce's claim to the Scottish throne. Roman Catholic and Protestant Martyrs burnt at the stake—during the 16th and early 17th centuries—for their beliefs. Wat Tyler was struck dead in 1381 by the Lord Mayor, helping to bring the Peasants Revolt to an end. *Stations:* Barbican. Cir.M. Farringdon. Cir.M.

■ **Somerset House,** Strand and Victoria Embankment 1D 83
✪✪ Like a huge palace around a central square, Somerset House was built 1776-86 in grand neo classical style by Sir William Chambers on the site of the 16th c. palace of the Duke of Somerset.
The building once housed the Navy Board, the Royal Academy and Royal Society, more recently the Inland Revenue and General Register Office.
The Courtyard with its fountain display, is now a public open space and events venue. The **Courtauld Gallery** occupies the Strand side. The Visitor Centre, Embankment Galleries, restaurants and 800ft. river front terrace make up the south side, a Navy Commissioners Barge is displayed in the original Water Gate entrance. *Admission charges,* Visitor Centre free. Open: 10 am to 6 pm. extended evenings for courtyard, river front terrace and restaurants. *Stations:* Temple. Cir.D. Charing Cross. B.N.

■ **Sotheby's,** 34/5 New Bond Street. 1C 80
Founded in 1744 it is one of the oldest and largest firms of fine art auctioneers. Sales of furniture, jewellery, silver, porcelain, pictures, books etc., held regularly except in August. Telephone 020 7293 5000 for details.
Station: Bond Street. Cen. J.

■ **South Bank Arts Centre.** 3E 83 ✪✪
One of Londons premier centres of cultural excellence on the site of the 1951 Festival of Britain. Visit the Royal Festival Hall, the National Theatre and BFI Southbank, each has a foyer open daily with cafes, bookshops and exhibitions; also here are the Hayward Gallery and BFI IMAX cinema. Spacious riverside terraces offer an extensive choice of restaurants and the South Bank Book Market. *Stations:* Embankment. B.Cir.D.N. Waterloo. B.J.N.

■ **Southwark Cathedral,** London Bridge. 3F 85 ✪✪
This fine Gothic edifice built upon a nunnery, was originally
the church of an Augustinian Priory, founded under Henry
I. John Harvard, founder of Harvard University, U.S.A., was
baptised here in 1607. Exactly 300 years later a chapel
and window were erected in his memory by Harvard
students. Fletcher, Massinger and Edmund
Shakespeare—brother of William—are buried here. Open
daily. *Station:* London Bridge. J.N.

■ **Spencer House,** 27 St. James's Place. 4D 81 ✪
London's finest surviving 18th century Town House, built
1756-66 for the first Earl Spencer, an ancestor of the late
Diana, Princess of Wales. *Admission Charge.* Open:
Sundays only 10.30 a.m. to 5.45 p.m. closed Aug. and
Jan. Access by guided tour only. *Station:* Green Park. P.V

■ **Spitalfields Market,** Commercial Street. 2D 75
This historic fruit and vegetable market is now the centre of
a renewed Spitalfields area with its restaurants, shops and
popular Sunday market.*Station:* Liverpool Street. Cen.Cir.M

■ **Staple Inn,** Holborn. 3F 71
Staple Inn was formerly one of the lesser Inns of Court and
described by Charles Dickens in his novel 'Edwin Drood'.
His Mr. Grewgious lived here, and so in real life did Dr.
Johnson. *Station:* Chancery Lane. Cen.

■ **Tate Britain,** Millbank. 5B 94 ✪✪✪
The national gallery of British art from 1500 to the present,
from the Tudors to the Turner prize. This most
comprehensive collection of British art in the world includes
works by Blake, Constable, Epstein, Gainsborough,
Hogarth, Lely, Kneller, Stubbs, the Pre Raphaelites,
Spencer, Moore, Hockney and most notably the Turner
bequest in its own wing, the Clore Gallery.
Also special exhibitions and retrospectives.
Open: 10 am to 6 pm daily, 10 am to 10 pm. Friday.
Closed Christmas Eve and Day, Boxing Day.
Station: Pimlico. V.

■ **Tate Modern,** Bankside. 3C 84 ✪✪✪
Housed in the transformed former Bankside Power Station
is the Tate's collection of international modern art from
1900 to the present. It includes works by over 200 artists
including Auerbach, Bacon, Braque, Cragg, Duchamp,
Giacometti, Matisse, Picasso, Riley, Rothko, Warhol and
many contemporary and controversial artists. Also special
exhibitions and retrospectives. Roof top restaurant with
panoramic views over the City of London.
Open: 10 am. to 6 pm. daily, 10 am to 10 pm. Friday and
Saturday. *Stations:* Southwark. J. Blackfriars. Cir.D.

■ **Temple,** Fleet Street. 1F 83 ✪✪
A complex of quiet squares and courts, of quaint corners, these precincts preserve a remarkable feel of 'old London'. Formerly the property of the Knights Templars—from 1184 to 1313—and then of the Knights of St. John of Jerusalem; it finally came into the possession of two Inns of Court—Inner Temple and Middle Temple. Open: Middle Temple Hall 10 am to 12 pm. and 3 to 4 p.m. Mon. to Fri. only. Temple Church generally open daily. All closed for public holidays. *Station:* Temple. Cir.D.

■ **Temple Bar,** Strand. 5F 71
Historically the western entrance to the City of London; when the Sovereign visits the City she is met here by the Lord Mayor of London, a Griffin Monument marks the site. *Station:* Temple Cir.D.
The imposing **Temple Bar Gate** designed by Wren in 1672 and removed in 1878, is now sited between St Paul's Cathedral and Paternoster Square. 5C 72
Station: St Paul's. C.

■ **Tower Bridge Exhibition.** Tower Bridge. 3D 87
✪✪✪ ✪   Discover the history of Tower Bridge, how it works, London in the 1890's, and enjoy the spectacular views from the 142 ft high walkways. Tower Bridge, one of the sights of London, was designed by Barry and Jones and completed in 1894, the two draw-bridges open to allow the passage of large ships, a bell rings before the bridge opens, halting all traffic.
Admission Charge. Open 10 am to 6 pm Summer months. 9.30 to 5.30 Winter months. Closed 24-26 December.
Stations: Tower Hill. Cir.D. Tower Gateway. DLR.

■ **Tower of London.** 2D 87 ✪✪✪ ✪
Built in part by William the Conqueror in 1078 as a fortress to guard the river approach to London, this is the most perfect example of a medieval castle in England, the outer walls being added later.
The White Tower contains, besides its collection of firearms and execution relics, the finest early-Norman chapel in this country. The famous Crown Jewels are housed in Waterloo Block. Elsewhere is the Royal Fusiliers Museum. Wall Walk gives good views over the Tower and River.
Anne Boleyn, Katherine Howard, Lady Jane Grey, Margaret Countess of Salisbury, Jane Viscountess Rochford, Robert Devereux Earl of Essex, were executed on Tower Green.
Admission Charge. Open *Summer:* 9 a.m. to 5.30 p.m. Tues. to Sat. 10 a.m. to 5.30 p.m. Sun. and Mon. *Winter:* 9 am to 4.30 pm. Tues to Sat. 10 am. to 4.30 pm. Sun. and Mon. Closed 24-25th December, New Year's Day.

To book tickets advance Tel. 0844 482 7799.
Stations: Tower Hill. Cir.D. Tower Gateway. DLR.

■ **Trafalgar Square.** 3A 82 ✪✪✪
Laid out as a war memorial and named after the victory of
Trafalgar, the Square was completed in 1841. Nelson's
Column, 170 ft. high overall, traditionally allowing Nelson a
view of the sea. The lions at the base are by Landseer,
facing Whitehall is a 17th-century equestrian statue of
Charles I, the Martyr King.   *Station:* Charing Cross. B.N.

■ **Trocadero,** Piccadilly Circus. 2F 81 ✪
A loud, fast and brash entertainment complex, just the sort
of thing children like !   Attractions have individual
admission charges. Open: Daily. Closed 25th Dec.
Station: Picadilly Circus. B.P.

■ **Two Temple Place,** 2 Temple Place. 1F 83
Extravangant neo-Gothic mansion built for William Waldorf
Astor. Displays periodic loan exhibitions. Open: (execept
during changes of exhibition) daily- but closed Tuesday.
Station: Temple. C.D

■ **University of London,** Russell Square. 2A 70
This Senate House, completed just before the Second
World War, contains the University Library and central
administration. Many of the Schools and Institutes
constituting the University, like University College, are
located nearby; with others throughout the London area,
and some beyond. *Station:* Russell Square. P.

■ **Victoria and Albert Museum,** Cromwell Road. 3A 90
✪✪✪ One of the worlds great museums of fine and
applied art. It illustrates artistic achievement and
craftsmanship throughout the centuries and is arranged
into two groups (a) Primary Collections—of style, period or
nationality. (b) Departmental Collections— sculpture,
textiles, woodwork, etc.
Many galleries now benefit from world class modern
presentation including the British Galleries, Medieval and
Renaissance Galleries, Ceramics, Jewellery, Sculpture and
Theatre Galleries. Special exhibitions occur throughout the
year. The museum incorporates the National Art Library.
Open 10 a.m. to 5.45 p.m. daily. To 10 pm. Fridays (note:
selected galleries after 6pm). Closed 24-26 December.
Station: South Kensington. Cir.D.P.

■ **Vinopolis,** Bankside. 3E 85
Exhibition and multi-media tour of the worlds wines, wine
tastings, shops, restaurants. Admission charge. Open
daily. *Station:* London Bridge. J.N.

■ **Wallace Collection,** Hertford House, Manchester Square.
4F 67 ✪ The most representative collection in England of

French 18th-century painting, sculpture, furniture and Sevres porcelain. It includes masterpieces by Rembrandt, Hals, Rubens, Reynolds, Gainsborough, Van Dyck, Velasquez and Titian; important collections of ceramics, goldsmiths' work, and European and Oriental arms and armour. Formed in the main by the third and fourth Marquesses of Hertford and the latter's son, Sir Richard Wallace. Open: Daily 10 a.m. to 5 p.m. Closed 24 -26 December.
Stations: Bond Street. Cen.J., Baker Street. B.Cir.J.M.

■ **Wellcome Collection,** 183 Euston Road. 5F 61
Explores the culture of medicine through the arts, sciences and history through both permanent and temporary exhibitions. The Welcome Library is one of the world's greatest collections for the study of the history and progress of medicine. Open: Tues. to Sat. 10am to 6pm. Thurs. to 10pm. Sun. 11 to 6. Library closed Sunday.
Station: Euston Square Cir.M.H

■ **Wellington Arch,** Hyde Park Corner. 5A 80
Designed by Decimus Burton in 1828. Originally a statue of Wellington stood on top, this was replaced by the present group when the Arch was moved from the entrance to Hyde Park. The frieze is based on the Elgin Marbles to be seen in the British Museum.
Admission Charge. Open: Visitor Centre Exhibition and Viewing Platform 10 am. to 5 pm. (4pm. winter months). Closed Mon. and Tues. also 24-26 Dec. 1st. Jan.
Station: Hyde Park Corner. P.

■ **Wellington Museum,** see Apsley House.

■ **Wesley's House, Chapel and Museum of Methodism**
City Road. 1A 74   John Wesley lived here for 12 years and died in this house in 1791. His own rooms and furniture are preserved, and the Museum contains a unique collection of his possessions. Wesley is buried in the graveyard behind the Chapel.
Admission Charge. Open 10 a.m. to 4 p.m. Mon. to Sat. Closed Bank Hols. Chapel is also open for Sunday service (House and Museum open after Sunday service until 1.45 pm). *Stations:* Old Street. N. Moorgate. Cir.M.N

■ **Westminster Abbey,** Parliament Square. 2B 94 ✪✪✪
One of the most interesting and historic religious buildings in England, its origins go back to the founding of an Augustinian monastery by St Dunstan c. AD 960, Edward the Confessor added a new Abbey church consecrated 1065. Rebuilding in the Gothic style began under Henry III in 1245, the Choir and east end being rededicated 1269. The nave (at 102ft England's highest Gothic vault) dates from the late 13th and early 14th centuries. Major

additions to the medieval work are the Henry VII Chapel 1503-19 with its awe inspiring fan vault roof and the twin West Towers - 18th century additions by Nicholas Hawksmoor, a pupil of Wren.

Until George III most of the Kings of England were buried within its precincts. Almost all have been crowned here; the only two exceptions being Edward V, who was murdered before he could be crowned, and the Duke of Windsor, Edward VI who abdicated in 1936.

Many famous men are buried in the Abbey, there is the well known Poets Corner, and the grave of the Unknown Warrior. The Abbey Museum in the outstanding Norman Undercroft shows the history and a remarkable collection of Royal and Noble effigies and death masks.

Open: Nave, Royal Chapels, Poets' Corner, Choir, and Statesmens' Aisle, Chapter House and Museum open Monday to Saturday. Cloisters open daily.
Admission Charge for sightseers.
Visiting subject to restrictions during special services and ceremonies. Open on Sundays for services only.
Stations: Westminster. Cir.D.J. St. James's Park. Cir.D.

■ **Westminster Cathedral,** Ashley Place. 3E 93 ✪✪
Opened in 1903, this is the foremost Roman Catholic Church in England. The architect, John Francis Bentley, who was influenced by the Christian Byzantine style of St Sophia at Constantinople, died a year before the building was completed. A lift serves the Campanile, which is 284 ft. high. In May 1982 Pope John Paul II celebrated the first mass ever by a Pope on English soil.
Open 7 a.m. to 7 p.m. daily. Admission Charge for lift to viewing gallery, open 9.30 am to 5 pm. Monday to Friday. 9.30 am to 6 pm weekends. *Station:* Victoria. Cir.D.V.

■ **Westminster Hall,** Parliament Square. 1B 94 ✪
The main surviving fragment of the old Palace of Westminster destroyed by fire in 1834. Erected in 1097 by William Rufus, it was rebuilt 1394-99 by Richard II who was responsible for the magnificent oak roof spanning the width of the Hall. Many famous State trials have taken place here; among them those of Charles I, Sir Thomas More, Guy Fawkes and Warren Hastings. Now used for great functions and for 'Lying in State'.
Normally accessible via tours of the Houses of Parliament, see above for details. *Station:* Westminster. Cir.D.J.

■ **Whitechapel Art Gallery,** Whitechapel High Street, 4E 75
Exhibitions of modern and contemporary art, and showcase for new artists. Established in 1901 to bring art to the then culturally deprived 'East End', The gallery is an important Arts and Crafts building.
Admission Charge. Open Tues. to Sun 11 a.m. to 6 p.m.

Thus. to 9 p.m. *Station:* Aldgate East. D.M.H.

■ **Whitehall.** 4B 82 ✪✪✪
Part of the original palace of Whitehall, this famous thoroughfare extends from Trafalgar Square southwards to Parliament Square. At the entrance to the Horse Guards Parade, mounted guards are on sentry duty.
Downing Street, home of the Prime Minister, is a turning off Whitehall near the Cenotaph, the principal monument in the centre of the road. Many Government Departments are housed here.
Stations: Charing Cross. B.N. Westminster. Cir.D.J.

PLACES OF INTEREST, MUSEUMS and ART GALLERIES in OUTER LONDON

NOTE: These items are all outside the central area map. Many can be most easily visited by taking an appropriate coach tour, see Conducted Coach Tours.

■ **Battle of Britain Museum,** also Bomber Command Museum. ✪ ✪ See **Royal Air Force Museum.**

■ **British Music Experience,** The 02 Arena, SE10.
An interactive display exploring the rise and importance of post war popular music, the groups and the stars.
Open: daily 11 am to 7.30 pm. *Station:* North Greenwich.

■ **Brunel Museum,** Railway Avenue, Rotherhithe SE16.
The history of the worlds first under river tunnel, also the lives of the Brunel's, father and son. *Admission Charge.*
Open: daily 10am. to 5pm. *Station:* Rotherhithe. O.

■ **Chartwell,** near Westerham, Kent ✪
For many years the country home of Sir Winston Churchill; the house is maintained as he left it, as is the studio where many of his paintings were executed. There are extensive gardens.   Now a National Trust Property.
Admission Charge. Open: Mid March to end October 11 a.m. to 5 p.m. Closed Mon. and Tues, (but open Tuesdays in July and August).

■ **Chessington World of Adventures,** Leatherhead Road, Chessington, Surrey. ✪ ✪   Theme Park and Fun Fair with over 100 attractions and rides; also zoo and skyway monorail. *Admission Charge:* Fully open at peak times. Zoo only at times. General enquiries 0871 663 4477.
Station: Chessington South by train from Waterloo.

■ **Chiswick House,** Burlington Lane W4 ✪
A fine example of Palladian architecture built by the Third Earl of Burlington in the late 1720's, its frontage composed of two double approach stairways flanking a classical portico at first floor level. The interior with its series of connected rooms designed by William Kent has paintings

by Kneller, Lely and Guido Reni. The garden laid out by Kent was a forerunner to the English Landscape Park. *Admission Charge*. Open: April to October 10 a.m. to 5 p.m. Monday, Tuesday, Wednesday, Sunday & Bank Holidays. *Station:* Chiswick by train from Waterloo.

■ **Cutty Sark,** Greenwich, SE10 ✪✪✪ ✪
Built in 1869, this was the fastest and most famous of the clipper sailing ships that raced to bring their tea cargoes to British ports. After complete restoration, the ships raised position enables visitors to walk underneath and examine the shape of the hull. Interpretive exhibitions explore the history of the ship and the tea trade, and includes the world's largest collection of Merchant Navy figureheads *Station:* Greenwich by train from Charing Cross or London Bridge. Or Docklands Light Railway to Cutty Sark Station. Or by riverboat from Westminster or Tower Piers.

■ **Docklands**
The Port of London was once one of the worlds largest ports occupying the banks of the River Thames from the Tower of London to Woolwich; during the 1960's and 70's industrial strife and new technologies bought about their decline and replacement by modern facilities at Tilbury.
      Since then some eight and a half square miles of derelict or underused land and water has undergone a remarkable transformation.
      Among the features of interest are St. Katharine Docks, Design Museum and Butlers Wharf, Hay's Galleria, Canary Wharf Financial Centre, New Billingsgate Fish Market, London City Airport, The Thames Barrier and the dockside ExCeL state-of-the-art international event venue and The O2 arena. **See also Museum of London Docklands.**

■ **Dulwich Picture Gallery,** College Road, SE21 ✪
An outstanding collection of Flemish, Italian and Dutch Art. Paintings by Ruisdael, Van de Velde, Cuyp, Van Dyck, Rembrandt, Rubens, Claude, Raphael, Veronese, Murillo and Poussin, it also contains British 17th and 18th century portraiture, including Gainsborough and Reynolds. Special exhibitions of great interest throughout the year.
Admission Charge. Open: Tues. to Fri. 10 am. to 5pm. Sat. and Sun. 11 am. to 5pm. Closed Mon. except Bank Holiday Mondays. Closed Christmas and New Year.
Stations: North Dulwich by train from London Bridge or West Dulwich from Victoria.

■ **Eltham Palace,** Court Yard, Etham. ✪✪✪
A unique and spectacular Art Deco house, built for the Courtaulds in 1936, linked to the Great Hall with its massive hammerbeam roof built in the 1470's and other remains of the Medieval Palace; set in beautiful gardens.
Admission Charge. Open Sun. to Wed. 10 a.m. to 5 p.m.

summer months. 10am to 4pm winter months on restricted days. Closed Christmas and all January.
Station: Eltham or Mottingham from Victoria +15 min walk.

■ **Emirates Air Line Cable Car**
A Cable car ride across the river Thames linking stations at Greenwich Peninsula and The Royal Victoria Docks for pedestrians and cyclists. Opens mid 2012.
Stations: North Greenwich J. Royal Victoria DLR

■ **Epping Forest,** Between Chingford and Epping
A relic of the ancient Royal hunting forest of Waltham. Now extending about 11 miles north/south, by 2-3 miles across, and managed by the City of London Corporation providing free public access at all times. Epping Forest Museum is in Queen Elizabeth's Hunting Lodge, Rangers Road, E14.
Station: Chingford by train from Liverpool Street.

■ **Estorick Collection of Modern Art,** 39a Canonbury Square, N1 A museum of modern Italian Art including the finest collection of Futurist Paintings outside Italy. *Admission Charge.* Open Wed to Sat. 11am to 6pm. Sun.12 to 5pm. Closed Mon. & Tues.
Station: Highbury & Islington. V.

■ **Fan Museum,** 12 Crooms Hill, Greenwich SE10
Is the world's first and only museum of fans; elegant displays in a fine early Georgian house with Orangery and landscape garden. *Admission Charge.* Open: 11 am. to 5 pm. Tues. to Sat. From 12 pm. Sundays. Closed Mon.
Station: As for Cutty Sark.

■ **Firepower, Museum of the Royal Artillery.** Royal Arsenal, Woolwich SE18 The story of Artillery and the history of the Royal Arsenal. *Admission Charge.* Open 10.30 am. to 6 pm. Tues. to Sat. Closed Sun. and Mon.
Station: Woolwich Arsenal from Charing Cross.

■ **Freud Museum,** 20 Maresfield Gardens, Hampstead NW3
The study of the founder of psychoanalysis is kept exactly as it was in his lifetime, including his library, antiquities and the famous couch. *Admission Charge.* Open: 12 am. to 5 pm. Wed. to Sun. *Station:* Swiss Cottage. J.

■ **Fulham Palace Museum,** Bishops Avenue, SW6
Illustrates the history of the Palace. The site, first acquired by Bishop Waldhere in 704, was the residence of the Bishops of London until 1973. *Admission Charge.*
Open: Sat. to Wed. 1 pm. to 4 pm. Closed Thurs and Fri.
Station: Putney Bridge. D.

■ **Greenwich,**
For **Discover Greenwich Visitor Centre** see Royal Naval College. See also Cutty Sark, National Maritime Museum, Queen's House and Royal Observatory.

■ **Hampton Court Palace,** Hampton, Middlesex ✪✪✪
Built by Cardinal Wolsey in 1515, and at that time the
largest and most magnificent palace in England, it aroused
Henry VIII's envy and concern. Ten years later it was
presented to him by the Cardinal, and from then until
George II, remained a favourite Royal residence.
Set around the three principal courtyards, visitors can
explore The Wolsey Rooms, Henry VIII's State
Appartments and Chapel, the extensive Tudor Kitchens,
William III's State and private apartments etc. The
Renaissance Picture Gallery displays important works from
the Royal Art Collection. There are over 60 acres of
grounds and gardens, which include the Privy Garden, the
Orangery by Wren and the famous Maze.
Admission Charge. Open: daily 10 am. to 6 pm. Summer
months.10am to 4.30pm winter months. Closed 24-26 Dec.
Station: Hampton Court by train from Waterloo stn.
Or in summer, by riverboat from Westminster Pier.

■ **Hampstead Heath,** Hampstead, NW3
A great tract of undulating, informal parkland, among its
many delights are Parliament Hill, with its kite flyers and
superb views over London. See also Kenwood.
Open daily. Station: Hampstead. N.

■ **Hogarth's House,** Hogarth Lane, W14.
The Queen Anne style country home of the artist Hogarth,
now a museum of his drawings and engravings.
Open: Tues. to Sun. 12 noon to 5 pm. Closed Mon.
Christmas and Easter. *Station:* Turnham Green. D. P.

■ **Horniman Museum,** 100 London Road, SE23. ✪ ✪
Home to the most comprehensive musical instrument
collection in Britain, the museum has an internationally
renowned anthropological collection and a popular Natural
History Gallery featuring rare fossils and natural
specimens. The gardens with their stunning views over
London are an award winning mix of garden types.
Open: 10.30 am. to 5.30 pm. daily. Closed 24-26 Dec.
Station: Forest Hill by train from Charing Cross or London
Bridge.

■ **Keats House,** Wentworth Place, Keats Grove, NW3.
Keats Regency home between 1818-20. Now a museum of
personal relics. Open: Summer 1 to 5 p.m. Tues. to Sun.
Winter 1 to 5 pm. Fri. to Sun. *Station:* Hampstead. N.

■ **Kenwood, Hampstead,** NW3 ✪✪
A classical style mansion set in 24 acres of parkland once
owned by the first Earl of Mansfield. Designed by Robert
Adam 1767-9 with additions by Saunders in 1795.
Bequeathed to the Nation by the late Lord Iveagh in 1927,
complete with his fine collection of paintings and furniture.

Lakeside open air concerts held in the summer. Open: daily 11.30 am. to 4 pm daily. Closed 24-26 Dec. 1st Jan. Park open 8 a.m. to dusk. *Station:* Archway N. then Bus.

■ **Kew Bridge Steam Museum,** Green Dragon Lane, Brentford. ✪ Worlds largest collection of steam pumping engines together with related exhibitions and events. *Admission Charge.* Open: 11 am. to 4 pm. Closed Mondays except Bank Holidays. 'In Steam' weekends and Bank Holidays. *Station:* Kew Bridge by train from Waterloo.

■ **Kew Gardens,** Royal Botanic Gardens, Kew, Surrey. ✪✪✪ Beautifully situated by the Thames; contain over 25,000 different species and varieties of trees shrubs and plants from all over the world in 300 acres of landscape. The great many special features include two museums, an art gallery dedicated to botanical art, a magnificent Palm House, Lily House, Rhododendron Walk, Kew Palace and Princess of Wales Conservatory. *Admission Charge.* Open: Daily from 9.30 am. Closed 24 and 25th December. *Stations:* Kew Gardens. D. or Kew Bridge by train from Waterloo. In summer, by riverboat from Westminster Pier.

■ **Legoland,** Windsor Park, Windsor , Berkshire. ✪ Theme park for children, built from and around the lego building block theme; rides, set display pieces and attractions in 150 acres of parkland. *Admission Charge.* Open: 10 am. to 5 pm. (to 7 pm. in Summer school Holidays). Closed Winter months. Tel. 0871 222 2001. *Stations:* Windsor and Eton Central from Paddington, via Slough; or Windsor and Eton Riverside from Waterloo; then Legoland shuttle bus.

■ **Museum of Childhood,** Cambridge Heath Road, Bethnal Green E2. ✪ ✪ This branch of the Victoria and Albert Museum has outstanding collections of toys, games, dolls and dolls' houses; also children's costume; many activities for children. Open: 10 a.m. to 5.45 p.m. daily. Closed 25-26 Dec. 1st Jan. *Station:* Bethnal Green. Cen.

■ **Museum of London Docklands,** West India Quay, Hertmere Road E14 Tells the story of London's river and the importance of its trading port from Roman times onwards; 2000 years of history explored in interactive displays and historic artifacts. *Admission charge.* Open 10 am. to 6 pm., daily. Closed 24-26 Dec. *Station:* West India Quay. DLR.

■ **Museum of Richmond,** Old Town Hall, Whittaker Avenue, Richmond. Illustrates the long history of Richmond. Open: 11 am. to 5 pm. Tues. to Sat. Closed Public Holidays. *Station:* Richmond. D. or by train from Waterloo.

■ **National Achives,** Ruskin Avenue, Kew, Richmond, Surrey TW9 4DU. Houses the National Archives

accumulated since the Norman Conquest, including records created and acquired by the government. The Education and Visitor Centre mounts exhibitions featuring the nation's most famous documents and unique items of historical interest.   Reading rooms are open to the public Wednesday, Friday and Saturday 9 am. to 5 pm. (last call for documents 4.15 pm.); Tuesday and Thursday 9 am. to 7 pm. (last call 5 pm.). Closed Sunday and Monday, Bank Holidays and also Saturdays on Bank Holiday weekends.
Stations: Kew Gardens. D. or Kew Bridge by train from Waterloo Main Line Station.

National Maritime Museum, Greenwich, SE10 ✪✪✪✪
The National Museum of our maritime history dealing with every aspect of ships and seafaring both in peace and war, from prehistory to today. Exhibitions tell the story of historical events and important people, exploration and the world's oceans.
Besides the collections of ships models and works of art there are 'hands-on' interactive galleries for children. See also Queen's House and Royal Observatory.
Open: 10 am. to 5 pm. daily.   *Station:* Greenwich by train from Charing Cross or London Bridge. Or Docklands Light Railway to Cutty Sark Station. Or by riverboat from Westminster or Tower Pier.

Osterley Park House, off Jersey Road, Isleworth.
A National Trust property. The house was begun in the 1560's as an Elizabethan Mansion for Sir Thomas Gresham, founder of the Royal Exchange. Later remodelled by both William Chambers and Robert Adam. Besides adding the portico, Adam designed the magnificent interiors and matching furniture. Outside are stables, parkland and the elevated M4 motorway !
Admission Charge.   Open: Wed. Thurs. Fri. Sat. & Sun. 12 pm to 4.30 p.m. Mar. to Oct. Park daily.
Station: Osterley. P.

Queen's House, National Maritime Museum, Greenwich, SE10.   ✪ Commissioned by James 1st, this Palace is a design by Inigo Jones, which, with his Banqueting House, Whitehall, marks the introduction of the classical ideals of Palladian architecture into England.
Notable for its Great Hall, a huge 40ft cube with a fine black-and-white marble floor and the elegant Tulip Stairs, the first geometric self-supporting spiral stair in Britain.
Displays the museums maritime fine art collection.
Open as the National Maritime Museum.

Ragged School Museum, Copperfield Road, E3
Illustrates the life of poor of the East End in Victorian London. Open: Wed. and Thurs.10 am to 5 pm. 1st Sunday in the month 2-5 pm. *Station:* Mile End.

■ **Rangers House,** Chesterfield Walk, Greenwich, SE10

This fine 18th. century house with its remarkable long gallery stands on the edge of Greenwich Park. It now houses the Wernher Collection of paintings and treasures, including medieval and Renaissance works of art. *Admission Charge.* Open: 11 a.m. to 4 p.m. Mon. Tues. Wed. & Sun. April to end Sept. Prebooked groups in the winter months. *Station:* see the National Maritime Museum.

■ **Richmond Park, Surrey.** ✪✪

An extensive Royal Park, first enclosed by Charles Ist. in 1637. This rolling landscape of forest trees and undergrowth, roamed by herds of deer, is big enough to get lost in. Isabella Plantation is a noted woodland garden. Open daily. *Stations:* Richmond. D. or North Sheen or Richmond, by train from Waterloo.

■ **Royal Air Force Museum,** Grahame Park Way, NW9.

✪✪ ✪ Portrays the dramatic history of military aviation and aircraft from World War 1 onwards.

Battle of Britain Hall with its collection of fighter planes vividly displays the events and those involved in the battle for supremacy of the sky in 1940.

Bomber Command Hall tells the story of the development of aerial bombing and displays many famous aircraft.

Milestones of Flight Hall illustrates the history of aviation from airships to supersonic flight.

Open: 10 a.m. to 6 p.m. daily. Grahame-White Factory Aircraft Collection 10 am to 12 pm and 1.30 pm to 6 pm daily. Closed 24-26 Dec. New Year's Day.

Station: Colindale. N.

■ **Royal Artillery Museum,** see Firepower.

■ **Royal Naval College,** Greenwich, SE10 ✪

Stands on the site of the 15th. century Palace of Placentia, birthplace of Henry VIII and his daughters Mary and Elizabeth. Rebuilt by a succession of architects including Wren, the palace became Greenwich Hospital in 1705;

(the naval equivalent of the Royal Hospital for soldiers at Chelsea); and afterwards, in 1873, a college for the higher education of Naval Officers and now houses the University of Greenwich and Trinity College of Music.

The Discover Greenwich Visitor Centre, King William Walk, SE10, the magnificent Chapel of 1789 by James 'Athenian' Stuart and the unique Painted Hall by Sir James Thornhill are all open to the public.

Open: normally 10 am. to 5 pm. daily, subject to functions. Closed Christmas. *Admission Charge.*

Station: See National Maritime Museum.

■ **Royal Observatory Greenwich,** Greenwich Park, SE10

✪✪✪✪ Part of the National Maritime Museum housed

in apartments built in 1675 by Wren for the first astronomer Royal. New interactive astronomy galleries and state-of-the-art planetarium help explain some of the mysteries of the universe. Home of Greenwich Mean Time and the Meridian Line, where you can stand with one foot in the east and one in the west ! and see the time-ball fall at 1 o'clock precisely.
Open hours as the National Maritime Museum.
Planetarium shows daily. Admission charges.

■ **Syon House,** London Road, Brentford, Middlesex. ✪
The summer home of the Duke of Northumberland, Syon was originally a monastery built by Henry V in 1415. Much later a new house was built on the site incorporating parts of the monastery. The 16th century Italianate style exterior remains largely unaltered, the interior was redesigned by Robert Adam in the 1760s with typical plasterwork, pillars and statues. There are many paintings, including portraits by Reynolds and Gainsborough. Gardens laid out by Capability Brown.
Admission Charge. Open: HOUSE: 11 a.m. to 5 p.m. Wed. Thurs. Sun. & Bank Holiday Mondays, end March to end Oct. GARDENS: Summer months daily 10.30 a.m. to 5 p.m. or dusk if earlier. Winter months weekends and New Year day only, 10.30 am. to 4 pm. Closed Christmas.
Stations: Gunnersbury. D. then bus. Or Brentford by train from Waterloo.

■ **Thames Barrier,** Barrier Approach, SE7
Built to save London from flooding, the Barrier consists of huge movable steel gates pivoted between concrete piers; hydraulic machinery can lift the gates from the riverbed in 30 minutes. On the south side an exhibition, audio-visual presentation and viewing facilities are open for the public.
Admission Charge. Open: 10.30 am. to 5 pm Thursday to Sunday and Bank Holidays. *Station:* Charlton by train from Charing Cross or London Bridge.

■ **Thorpe Park,** Staines Road, Chertsey, Surrey ✪
Theme Park and fun fair with over 70 attractions around a lakeland setting; also working farm and craft shops.
Admission Charge. Open: times vary; closed winter months. *Station:* Staines by train from Waterloo, then bus.

■ **William Morris Gallery,** Lloyd Park, Forest Road, E17
Devoted to the life and work of William Morris, his followers and the Morris Company.
Open: 10 am. to 5 pm Wednesday to Sunday. Closed Public Holidays. *Station:* Tottenham Hale. V.

■ **Warner Bros. Studio Tour - The Making of Harry Potter,** Leavesden Studios, South Way, Watford
Behind the scenes tour of the most successful film series

of all time, the sets, costume, animatronics, special effects. Tickets must be booked in advance via www.wbstudiotour.co.uk.

■ **Wimbledon Lawn Tennis Museum,** All England Tennis Club, Church Road, SW19.
The history of tennis, displays of trophies and features on tennis stars. *Admission Charge.* Open: 10 am. to 5 pm. daily; varies during The Championships.
Stations: Southfields D. Wimbledon Park D.

■ **Windsor Castle,** Windsor, Berkshire. ✪✪✪
A royal residence since William the Conqueror first built a wood and earth castle here; this massive castle is now the largest in England and dominates the town skyline. When Her Majesty, Queen Elizabeth is here, the Royal Standard flies from the Round Tower. The State Apartments, rebuilt by Charles II, and richly furnished, contain many works of art by the Old Masters from the Royal Art Collection.
St. George's Chapel, a superb example of Perpendicular architecture, was begun for Edward IV as a private chapel for Knights of the Garter. Windsor Great Park with its famous Long Walk, and Virginia Water, once formed part of the ancient Royal Forest of Windsor.
Changing of the Guard takes place at 11am Mon. to Sat. in summer months, on alternate days winter months.
Admission Charge: Open: CASTLE & ST GEORGE'S CHAPEL: Daily 9.45 a.m. to 5.15 p.m. (to 4.15 p.m. Nov. to Feb.). Notes: closed on certain days throughout the year for official or Royal functions, for details telephone 020 7766 7304. St. George's Chapel is closed to visitors on Sundays.
Stations: Windsor and Eton Central from Paddington, via Slough; or Windsor and Eton Riverside from Waterloo Main Line Stations.

PAGEANTRY

■ **CEREMONY OF THE KEYS**
Tower of London, continues after 700 years to be a 10 p.m. nightly event. The Chief Yeoman Warder—in scarlet coat, Tudor bonnet, and carrying a lantern—with foot Guard escort, locks up the several gates.
For admission write to: The Ceremony of the Keys, Waterloo Block, H.M. Tower of London, EC3N 4AB enclosing a stamped and addressed envelope.

■ **CHANGING OF THE GUARD** ✪✪✪ ✪
BUCKINGHAM PALACE. Takes place at 11.30 on a variable timetable of alternate days, or daily when possible during the Summer months. For up-to-date information

telephone 020 7766 7300, see Visit London page 45 or the notice board at the Buckingham Palace gates.

The ceremony is carried out by one of the five regiments of Foot Guards, marching to the band, and resplendent in scarlet tunics and black bearskins (cancelled in very wet weather).

HORSE GUARDS Courtyard, Whitehall. Daily at 11 a.m. (Sundays, 10 a.m.) Ceremony by one of the two regiments of Household Cavalry either the Royal Horse Guard in blue tunics, or the Life Guards in scarlet. Traditional breastplates are worn by both regiments.

■ LORD MAYOR'S SHOW
A colourful annual procession (usually second Saturday November) when the newly-elected Lord Mayor drives in his gilded state coach, drawn by six horses to the Law Courts to take the oath.

■ OPENING OF THE ROYAL COURTS OF JUSTICE
The first Monday in October, all Her Majesty's Judges and members of the Bar—in State robes and full-bottomed wigs—attend a service in Westminster Abbey. Then, led by the Lord Chancellor, they walk in procession to the House of Lords; and after lunching there drive to the Law Courts. The first Motion of the year, taken in his court by the Lord Chancellor, constitutes the opening of all the courts.

■ REMEMBRANCE SUNDAY
Annually, on the Sunday nearest November 11th, the Queen, the Prime Minister, Ministers, and members of the Opposition, take up their places by the Cenotaph, for the 11 a.m. two minutes silence The Queen leads the laying of wreaths in memory of those killed in battle since 1914.

■ STATE OPENING OF PARLIAMENT
After each General Election, and also annually normally at the end October or early November.

The Queen wearing her crown and robes of state, and escorted by Life Guards and Royal Horse Guards, is driven in her state coach along the Mall and Whitehall to the Houses of Parliament. There, in the House of Lords, she makes her speech from the throne, to both the Lords and Members of Parliament, who will have been summoned from the House of Commons.

■ TROOPING THE COLOUR ✪✪✪
Every June, on the Saturday nearest to the Queen's official birthday. This ceremony—dating from 1750—takes place on the Horse Guards Parade. The Queen, accompanied by Household Cavalry, and Guardsmen, travels there from Buckingham Palace and back again, to the strains of martial music.

BRASS RUBBING

■ **London Brass Rubbing Centre.**
St. Martin in the Fields, St. Martin's Place. 2B 82
Open 10 a.m. to 6p.m. Monday to Wednesday. 10 am. to 9
pm Thursday to Saturday. 11.30 am. to 5 pm. Sunday.

VIEWPOINTS

■ For panoramic viewpoints visit the following

City Hall -4C86	St. Paul's Cathedral -5C72
Golden Jubilee Bridges -3D83	South Bank -3D83
London Eye -5D83	Tower Bridge Walkway -3D87
Millennium Bridge -2D85	Wellington Arch -5A80
Monument, The -1A86	Westminster Cathedral
Oxo Tower Wharf -2A84	-3E93

WALKS IN CENTRAL LONDON

**Places in blue type appear in alphabetical order from
page 2, together with description and admission times.**

■ One day: Starting at Buckingham Palace a walk along
Birdcage Walk brings you to Parliament Square, with
Westminster Abbey, the Houses of Parliament and Big
Ben. Leaving Westminster Bridge on the right; walk up
Whitehall past Downing Street and the Horse Guards to
Trafalgar Square, where are Nelson's Column and the
National Gallery. If your interests are historical and
architectural take a bus along the Strand past the Law
Courts to Fleet Street and St. Paul's Cathedral, and from
there a bus to the Monument. A walk along Eastcheap and
Great Tower Street brings you to the Tower of London.

If you prefer to see the West End shopping centre, take a
bus from Trafalgar Square through Piccadilly Circus to
Regent Street, walk north up to Oxford Circus, then turn
left- west along Oxford Street, down Bond Street, and then
left again at Piccadilly, which will bring you back to
Piccadilly Circus, passing Burlington Arcade.

■ Two days: Take the underground to Tower Hill and nearby
is the Tower of London with Tower Bridge beyond. Across
the river are seen H.M.S. Belfast and the spires of
Southwark Cathedral.
A walk along Lower Thames Street and past Old
Billingsgate Fish Market brings you to the Monument, from
which King William Street leads to the heart of the City,
with the Bank of England, the Mansion House and the
Royal Exchange among many other famous buildings.
From here St. Paul's Cathedral is a short bus ride or walk.
Almost any bus going down Ludgate Hill continues

through what was once the newspaper centre of Fleet Street to the Strand. On the right are the Royal Courts of Justice, and in the middle of the road the island churches of St. Clement Danes and St. Mary-le-Strand.

The Strand opens into Trafalgar Square, with its fountains, Nelson's Column, Admiralty Arch and the National Gallery. Any bus down Whitehall passes the entrance to the Horse Guards where two mounted sentries are on guard. On the left is Inigo Jones's Banqueting House, from which Charles I was led to his execution. Government offices line Whitehall, and on the right is the famous Downing Street. The Cenotaph is slightly beyond and soon Whitehall opens out into Parliament Square.

Here, the Houses of Parliament, St. Margaret's Church and Westminster Abbey form an impressive group. Take a bus proceeding along Victoria Street—on the right is the New Scotland Yard building, on the left rises the Campanile of Westminster Cathedral—to Victoria Station, and walk along Buckingham Palace Road to Buckingham Palace; where the Royal Standard will be flying if Her Majesty the Queen is in residence. Walk along the tree-lined Mall and skirt the battlemented walls of St. James's Palace, Pall Mall, with its well-known clubs, is soon reached. Farther along Pall Mall is Waterloo Place, with the Duke of York's Column in the centre, and by turning left up Regent Street you come to Piccadilly Circus. A bus up Regent Street to Oxford Circus, and another along Oxford Street to Museum Street, brings you near to the British Museum. From here it is only a short distance to London University.

Three days: The same route should be followed, but more time devoted to the Tower of London, St. Paul's Cathedral, The National Gallery in Trafalgar Square, Westminster Abbey and the British Museum. Then take the Central Line underground from Tottenham Court Road to Queensway, and walk south along the Broad Walk through Kensington Gardens. On the right lies Kensington Palace, on the left the Round Pond. On reaching Kensington Road turn left to the Albert Memorial, the Royal Albert Hall and the museums: the Science Museum, the Natural History Museum, and the Victoria and Albert Museum. Close by is the Roman Catholic Brompton Oratory and the busy shopping centres of Brompton Road and Knightsbridge.

Four or more days: More time should be given to the places already mentioned that interest you most- but while in the Strand, Lincoln's Inn Fields and The Temple should be visited.
A short distance from Oxford Street, opposite Bond Street Station, is the Wallace Collection in Manchester Square. From Baker Street, nearby, buses go to Regent's Park,

with its London Zoo.

TOURIST INFORMATION

■ VISIT LONDON
Visit London Line, telephone 08701 566366, Visit London's tourist information and accommodation booking service. www.visitlondon.com

■ TOURIST INFORMATION CENTRES

City of London Information Centre, St. Paul's Churchyard, 020-7332 1456 –5C 72 Open 9.30 am to 5.30 pm Mon to Sat 10 am to 4 pm Sun. Closed 25-26 Dec.

Greenwich Tourist Information Centre, Pepys House, 2 Cutty Sark Gardens, SE 10, 087 0608 2000. Open daily 10 am to 5 pm. Closed 25-26 Dec.

■ TOURIST DISCOUNT CARDS
London Pass, combines admittance to over 55 visitor attractions, tours and cruises. The London Transport Travelcard is an optional extra. Available from the Britain & London Visitor Centre and **www.londonpass.com**

■ RIVER THAMES BOAT TRIPS ✪✪
London River Services Tel: 020 7941 2400

FROM WESTMINSTER PIER **1C 94**   EMBANKMENT PIER **3D 83** and LONDON EYE PIER **5D 83**
Regular trips to Tower of London, Greenwich and Thames Barrier downstream: also services to Kew Gardens, Richmond and Hampton Court upstream.
FROM TOWER PIER **3C 86**
Regular trips to Greenwich and Thames Barrier downstream; and Westminster upstream; also across the river to HMS Belfast.

■ CANAL TRIPS ✪
Jason's Trip, Little Venice, 2D 65 For bookings, telephone 020 7286 3428.
*Jenny Wren Canal Trips, Camden Lock, Camden High Street, NW1. For bookings telephone 020 7485 4433.
London Waterbus Company, Little Venice, 2D 65 and
 * Camden Lock, Camden High Street, NW1
 020 7482 2550

■ ROUND LONDON SIGHTSEEING TOURS ✪✪
Circular tours run from the designated bus stops at many central locations, (Piccadilly Circus, Trafalgar Square etc.). They tour a variety of routes around the main tourist areas, and provide a hop-on, hop-off service for visiting the attractions on the route, spoken commentary, and usually open top buses.

Original London Sightseeing Tour 020 8877 1722
Big Bus Company 020 7233 9533

■ **CONDUCTED COACH TOURS** ✪
Tours are guide conducted in luxury coaches to some of
the famous show places in and around London. All seats
bookable. For information and to reserve seats apply to a
Tourist or Travel Information Centre, Victoria Coach Station
or travel agents.
* Outside Central London area mapped.

TRANSPORT INFORMATION

■ **BUSES AND UNDERGROUND RAILWAY**
For enquiries on buses, underground trains and Docklands
Light Railway services.
24 hour travel information Tel: 0843 222 1234.
www.tfl.gov.uk

■ **TRAVEL INFORMATION CENTRES**
At Piccadilly Circus 2E 81, King's Cross St. Pancras 3B 62
and Liverpool Street 3B 74 Underground Stations. Also
Euston 3E 61 and Victoria 3C 92 Main Line Railway
Stations, Victoria Coach Station 5B 92 and Heathrow
Airport Terminals 1,2,3 Underground Station.

■ **TRAVELCARDS**
On sale at Underground Stations, Transport for London
Travel Information Centres and Main Line Railway Stations.
Travelcards give access to London Buses, Underground
Trains and Tramlink, also the Docklands Light Railway and
most parts of the Rail system within Greater London.
　Travelcards are good value, save time as well as the
need to buy separate tickets for each journey. Travelcards
can be bought for 1 day, 3 days or 7 days (photograph
required for 7 days). They cannot be used on coach tours.
　Oyster Card (deposit required) is an alternative that
enables you to pre-pay for your journeys at reduced rates.

■ **DOCKLANDS LIGHT RAILWAY**
Enquiries 0843 222 1234.
From Bank Station 5F 73 or Tower Gateway Station 1E 87
Lewisham Line for Canary Wharf, Cutty Sark and
Greenwich. Woolwich Arsenal Line for London City Airport.
Beckton Line for ExCeL.

■ **TAXIS**
Scale of charges is shown in each taxi-cab.

■ **COACHES**
Coaches travel from London to most Towns and Cities,
seats must be booked in advance.

Victoria Coach Station, 164 Buckingham Palace Road.
5B 92. Open daily 7 am to 10 pm.
National Express Coach Service information
Tel: 08717 81 81 81   for advice, ticket ammendments,
refunds and cancellations.

■ **GREEN LINE COACHES**
Connecting Central London with towns in the surrounding
counties. Green Line Coach Station, Bulleid Way,
Eccleston Bridge. Tel: 0844 801 7261. 4C 92

■ **MAIN LINE RAILWAY TERMINI**
Note: Through tickets for any station, irrespective of region,
may be obtained from any station booking office. Seats and
sleeping berths may be reserved in the same way.

■ NATIONAL RAIL ENQUIRIES 24 hours. daily
Tel. 08457 48 49 50

Blackfriars 1B 84. Cannon Street 1F 85. Charing Cross 3C
82. Euston 3E 61. Fenchurch Street 1C 86. King's Cross
2B 62. Liverpool Street 3B 74. London Bridge 4A 86.
Marylebone 1C 66. Paddington 4F 65. St. Pancras
International 2B 62. Victoria 4C 92. Waterloo 5F 83.

■ **EUROSTAR**
Through services direct to Paris and Brussels via the
Channel Tunnel.
Information and Bookings Telephone 08432 186186.
St. Pancras International Station 2B 62.

■ **AIRPORTS**
Gatwick, Gatwick, West Sussex. 0844 335 1802
Heathrow, Hounslow, Middlesex. 0844 335 1801
London City, Silvertown, E16 020 7646 0088
Luton, Luton, Bedfordshire. 01582 405100
Stansted, Stansted, Essex. 0844 335 1803

■ **AIRPORT LINKS**
■ **Gatwick-Central London**
  1. Gatwick Express, from Victoria Station.
  2. National Express Coach, from Victoria Coach Station.

■ **Heathrow-Central London**
  1. Heathrow Express, from Paddington Station.
  2. Heathrow Connect, from Paddington Station.
  3. Underground Train, Piccadilly Line fron central London.
  4. National Express Coach from Victoria Coach Station.

■ **London City-Cental London**
  Docklands Light Railway from Bank or Tower Gateway.

■ **Luton-Central London**
  1. Rail services from either St. Pancras International
     Station, Farringdon, City Thameslink or Blackfriars

Stations to Luton Airport Parkway for connecting
Shuttlebus service.
2. Greenline Coach 757 from Buckingham Palace Road,
beside Victoria Station.

■ **Stansted-Central London**
1. Stansted Express from Liverpool Street Station.
2. National Express Coach service from Victoria Coach
Station.

■ **Heathrow-Gatwick-Stansted**
National Express Coach airport transfer service.

■ **LOST PROPERTY**
Property lost on Buses, London Underground, London
Overground and black taxi cabs is forwarded to —

TfI Lost Property Office, 200 Baker Street, NW1 5RZ –1E
67. Open 09.30-16.00 Monday to Friday, closed Bank
Holidays. 0845 330 9882.

Property lost on boats, trams and minicabs is held by the
operator.

PLACES OF WORSHIP

■ **BAPTIST**
Bloomsbury Central Church, Shaftesbury Avenue. 4B 70
Station: Tottenham Court Road
Gower Street Memorial Chapel, Shaftesbury Avenue. 5B
70 *Station:* Tottenham Court Road
Metropolitan Tabernacle, Elephant & Castle 4C 96 *Station:*
Elephant & Castle
Westminster, Horseferry Road 3A 94 *Station:* St. James's
Park

■ **CHRISTIAN SCIENCE**
Second Church of Christ, Scientist, 104 Palace Gardens
Terrace, W8 3A 76 *Station:* Notting Hill Gate

■ **CHURCH OF ENGLAND**
All Saints, Margaret Street. 4D 69
Station: Oxford Circus
All Souls, Langham Place. 3C 68
Station: Oxford Circus
Chapel Royal, St. James's Palace. 4E 81
Station: Green Park
Christ Church Spitalfields, Commercial Street. 2D 75
Station: Aldgate East
St. George (Hanover Square), St. George Street. 1C 80
Station: Oxford Circus
St Giles-in-the-Fields, St. Giles High Street. 4A 70
Station: Tottenham Court Road
St James's, Piccadilly. 2E 81
Station: Piccadilly Circus

St Margaret's, Westminster. 1B 94
Station: Westminster
St. Martin-in-the- Fields, St. Martin's Place. 2B 82
Station: Charing Cross
St. Marylebone, Marylebone Road. 1A 68
Station: Baker Street
St. Paul's, Covent Garden. 1C 82
Station: Covent Garden
St. Paul's Cathedral, Ludgate Hill. 5C 72
Station: St Paul 's
Southwark Cathedral, Cathedral Street. 3F 85
Station: London Bridge
Westminster Abbey, Parliament Square. 2B 94
Station: Westminster

- **CHURCH OF SCOTLAND**
Crown Court Church, Russell Street. 5C 70
Station: Holborn
St. Columba's, Pont Street. 3D 91
Stations: Knightsbridge, Sloane Square

- **DANISH CHURCH**
Danish Church, Regent's Park. 2B 60
Station: Regent's Park

- **DUTCH CHURCH**
Dutch Church, Austin Friars. 4A 74   *Station:* Bank

- **FRENCH PROTESTANT**
Eglise Protestante, Française de Londres,
9 Soho Square. 4F 69
Station: Tottenham Court Road

- **GREEK ORTHODOX**
St. Sophia's, Moscow Road. 1B 76   *Station:* Bayswater

- **INDEPENDENT EVANGELICAL**
Westminster Chapel, Buckingham Gate. 2E 93
Station: St James's Park

- **INTERDENOMINATIONAL**
American Church in London, 79 Tottenham Court Road,
2E 69   *Station:* Goodge Street

- **JEWISH**
Bevis Marks Synagogue, 4C 74   *Station:* Aldgate
Central Synagogue, Gt. Portland Street. 2C 68
Station: Gt. Portland Street
New West End Synagogue, 10 St. Petersburgh Place
2B 76   *Station:* Queensway
*Spanish and Portuguese Synagogue, St Jame's Gardens,
W11 *Station:* Holland Park
West London Synagogue (Reform), 34 Upper Berkeley
Street. 5D 67   *Station:* Marble Arch

50

■ **LUTHERAN**
St. Anne & St Agnes (Lutheran) Church, **Gresham Street.**
4D 73   *Station:* St. Paul's

■ **METHODIST**
Central Hall, Tothill Street, Westminster 1A 94
Stations: Westminster, St. James's Park
Chiltern Street Welsh Methodist, Chiltern Street
2F 67   *Station:* Baker Street.
(Last Sunday in month 6.30 pm only)
Hinde Street Church, Theyer Street. 4A 68
Station: Bond Street
Wesley's Chapel, City Road. 1A 74
Stations: Moorgate, Old Street.

■ **MOSLEM**
London Central Mosque, Regent's Park. 4C 58
Station: Baker Street

■ **ROMAN CATHOLIC**
Church of the Immaculate Conception, **Farm Street,**
Berkeley Square. 2B 80
Stations: Green Park, Bond Street
French Catholic Church of Notre Dame de France,
Leicester Place, off Leicester Square. 1A 82
Station: Leicester Square
Oratory, The, Brompton Road. 3B 90
Station: South Kensington
St. George's Cathedral, St. George's Road. 2A 96
Station: Lambeth North
St. James's, Spanish Place, Manchester Square. 3A 68
Station: Bond Street
St Patrick Catholic Church, 21 Soho Square.
5A 70   *Station:* Tottenham Court Road
Ukranian Catholic Cathedral, Duke Street. 1A 80
Station: Bond Street
Westminster Cathedral, Ashley Place. 3D 93
Station: Victoria

■ **RUSSIAN ORTHODOX CHURCH IN EXILE**
All Saints Cathedral, Ennismore Gardens, SW7.
1B 90   *Station:* South Kensington

■ **SALVATION ARMY**
Regent Hall, 275 Oxford Street. 5C 68
Station: Oxford Circus

■ **SOCIETY OF FRIENDS (QUAKERS)**
Friends House, Euston Road. 5F 61
Station: Euston Square
Toynbee Hall, 28 Commercial Street. 3E 75
Station: Aldgate East
Westminster Meeting House, 52 St. Martin's Lane. 1B 82
Station: Leceister Square

■ **SWEDISH**
Swedish Church, 11 Harcourt Street. 3C 66
Stations: Edgware Road, Marylebone

■ **SWISS CHURCH**
Eglise Suisse de Londres, 79 Endell Street. 4B 70
Station: Tottenham Court Road

■ **UNITARIAN**
Essex Church, Palace Gardens Terrace. 3A 76
Station: Notting Hill Gate

■ **UNITED REFORMED**
Christ Church and Upton Chapel, Westminster Bridge
Road. 2F 95   *Station:* Lambeth North
City Temple, Holborn Viaduct. 3A 72 *Station:* St. Paul's
Lumen URC, Regent Square. 4C 62
Stations: King's Cross, St. Pancras

■ **WELSH**
Welsh Baptist Chapel, 30 Eastcastle Street. 4E 69
Station: Oxford Circus.

*Outside Central London area mapped.

■ ███████████ **TICKETS** ███████████

Tickets should be bought from either the venue or a
reputable ticket agency.   Popular shows are often sold out
weeks or months ahead, it is however possible to queue for
'returns'- returned tickets on the night of performance;
these are available only from the venue box office.

■ The **Half Price Ticket Booth** can also offer tickets on the
day of performance.   Beware of ticket touts who may
approach you in such queues.

■ **Theatre, Concert, Events and Sports Ticket Agencies:**
Keith Prowse: 0844 209 0382
Stargreen: 020 7734 8932
Ticketmaster: 0844 844 0444
Half Price Ticket Booth, Leicester Square 2A 82
(open to Personal callers only).

■ ███████████ **WEST END CINEMAS** ███████████

Nearest station shown in italics.

Apollo, Regent Street. 2F 81 *Piccadilly Circus*
Barbican, 1 Silk Street. 2E 73 *Barbican, Moorgate*
BFI Southbank, South Bank. 3E 83 *Waterloo*
*Chelsea Cinema, 206 King's Road. SW3. *Sloane Square.*
Cine Lumiere,   Queensberry Place 4F 89
    South Kensington
*Cineworld Chesea, 279 Kings Road. SW3 *Sloane Square*
*Cineworld Fulham Road, SW10 *South Kensington*
Cineworld Haymarket, Haymarket. 2F 81 *Piccadilly Circus*

Cineworld Trocadero, Trocadero Centre. 2F 81
Curzon Mayfair, Curzon Street. 4B 80 *Green Park*
Curzon Millbank, Millbank. 5B 94 *Pimlico*
Curzon Soho, Shaftesbury Avenue. 5A 70
   Piccadilly Circus
Empire, Leicester Square. 1A 82 *Leicester Square*
ICA Nash House, The Mall. 3A 82 *Charing Cross*
IMAX BFI Imax, Waterloo. 4F 83 *Waterloo*
National Film Theatre, See BFI Southbank
Odeon Covent Garden, Shaftesbury Avenue. 5A 70
   Leicester Square
*Odeon Kensington High Street, Kensington High
   Street. 2A 88 *High Street Kensington*
Odeon Leicester Square, 2A 82 *Leicester Square*
Odeon Marble Arch, Marble Arch. 5E 67 *Marble Arch*
Odeon Mezzanine, see Odeon Leicester Square
Odeon Panton Street, Panton Street. 2A 82
   Piccadilly Circus
Odeon Tottenham Court Road, Tottenham Court
   Road. 3F 69 *Tottenham Court Road*
Odeon West End, Leicester Square. 2A 82
   Leicester Square
Odeon, Whiteleys Centre, Queensway. 5C 64 *Queensway*
Prince Charles, Leicester Place, off Leicester Square.
   1A 82 *Leicester Square*
Renoir, Brunswick Square. 1C 70 *Russell Square*
Screen on Baker Street, Baker Street. 2E 67 *Baker Street.*
*Screen on the Green, Islington Green, N1. *Angel*
Vue West End, Leicester Square. 1A 82
   Leicester Square

*Outside Central London area mapped.

WEST END THEATRES, OPERA & BALLET HOUSES

Nearest station shown in italics.
Adelphi, Strand. 2C 82 *Charing Cross*
Aldwych, Aldwych. 1D 83 *Covent Garden*
Ambassadors, West Street. 5B 70 *Leicester Square*
Apollo, Shaftesbury Avenue. 1F 81 *Piccadilly Circus*
Apollo Victoria, Wilton Road. 3D 93 *Victoria*
Arts, 6 Great Newport Street. 1B 82 *Leicester Square*
Barbican, Silk Street. 2E 73 *Barbican, Moorgate*
Bloomsbury, Gordon Street. 5F 61. *Euston Square*
Britten Opera Theatre, Royal College of Music,
   Prince Consort Road. 2F 89 *South Kensington*
Cambridge, Earlham Street. 5B 70 *Leicester Square*
Cochrane, Southampton Row 3D 71 *Holborn*
Cockpit, Gateforth Street. 1B 66 *Marylebone*
Coliseum, St. Martin's Lane. 2B 82 *Leicester Square*
Comedy, Panton Street. 2A 82 *Piccadilly Circus*
Cottesloe, See National

Criterion, Piccadilly. 2F 81 *Piccadilly Circus*
Dominion, Tottenham Court Rd. 4A 70 *Tottenham Ct. Rd*
Donmar Warehouse, Earlham Street. 5B 70
    Leicester Square
Drury Lane, Catherine Street. 5D 71 *Covent Garden*
Duchess, Catherine Street. 1D 83 *Covent Garden*
Duke of York's, St. Martin's Lane. 2B 82
    Leicester Square
English National Opera, see Coliseum
Fortune, Russell Street. 5C 70 *Covent Garden*
Garrick, Charing Cross Road. 2B 82 *Leicester Square*
Gielgud, Shaftesbury Avenue. 1F 81 *Piccadilly Circus*
Globe, See Shakespeare's Globe
Greenwood, Weston Street. 5A 86 *London Bridge*
*Hackney Empire, 291 Mare Street. E8
    Hackney Central
Haymarket, Haymarket. 2A 82 *Piccadilly Circus*
Her Majesty's, Haymarket. 3F 81 *Piccadilly Circus*
ICA Carlton House Terrace 3A 82 *Charing Cross*
Jermyn Street, Jermyn Street. 2E 81 *Piccadilly Circus*
*Labatt's Apollo Hammersith, Queen Caroline
    Street, W6. *Hammersmith*
Leicester Square, Leicester Place, Leicester Square.
    IA 82 *Leicester Square*
Lyceum, Wellington Street. ID 83 *Charing Cross*
Lyric, Shaftesbury Avenue. 1F 81 *Piccadilly Circus*
*Lyric Hammersmith, King Street. W6 *Hammersmith*
Lyttelton, See National
Menier, Southwark Street, 4E 85 *London Bridge*
National, Upper Ground, South Bank. 3E 83 *Waterloo*
New Diorama, 15-16 Triton Street. 5D 61 *Gt. Portland St.*
New London, Drury Lane. 4C 71 *Covent Garden*
New Players, The Arches, off Villiers Street. 3C 82
    Charing Cross, Embankment
Noel Coward, St. Martins Lane. 1B 82 *Leicester Square*
Novello, Aldwych. 1D 83 *Covent Garden*
Old Vic, Waterloo Road. 5A 84 *Waterloo*
Old Vic Tunnels, Via Lower Marsh. 1F 95 *Waterloo*
Olivier, See National
Open Air, Regent's Park. 4F 59 *Baker Street.*
Palace, Shaftesbury Avenue. 5A 70 *Leicester Square*
Palladium, Argyll Street. 5D 69 *Oxford Circus*
Place, The, Duke's Road.. 4A 62 *Euston*
Peacock, Portugal Street. 5D 71 *Holborn*
Phoenix, Charing Cross Road. 5A 70 *Tottenham Court Rd.*
Piccadilly, Denman Street. 1E 81 *Piccadilly Circus*
Playhouse, Northumberland Avenue, 3C 82
    Charing Cross
Prince Edward, Old Compton Street 5F 69
    Leicester Square
Prince of Wales, Coventry Street. 2F 81

Piccadilly Circus
Queens, Shaftesbury Avenue. 1F 81 *Piccadilly Circus*
Robin Howard Dance Theatre, Duke's Road.
    4A 62 *Euston*
Royal Court, Sloane Square. 5F 91
Royal National Theatre, See National
Royal Opera House, Covent Garden. 5C 70 *Covent*
    Garden
*Sadler's Wells, Rosebery Avenue. EC1 *Angel*
St. Martin's, West Street. 1B 82 *Leicester Square*
Savoy, Strand. 2D 83 *Embankment*
Shaftesbury, Shaftesbury Avenue. 4B 70
    Tottenham Court Road
Shakespears's Globe, Bankside. 3D 85
    London Bridge
Shaw, Euston Road. 3A 62 *Euston*
Siobhan Davis Dance Centre, St. George's Road.
    3B 96 *Elephant & Castle*
Soho Theatre and Writers Centre, Dean St. 5F 69
    Oxford Circus
Theatre Royal Drury Lane, see Drury Lane
Theatre Royal Haymarket, see Haymarket
*Theate Royal Stratford East, Gerry Raffles
    Square. E15 *Stratford*
Trafalgar Studios, Whitehall. 3B 82 *Charing Cross*
Unicorn, Tooley Street, 4C 86 *London Bridge*
Union, Union Street. 4C 84 *Southwark*
Vanburgh, RADA, Malet Street. 1A 70 *Goodge Street*
Vaudeville, Strand. 2C 82 *Embankment*
Victoria Palace, Victoria Street. 3C 92 *Victoria*
Waterloo East, Brad Street, 4A 84 *Southwark*
Wilton's Music Hall, Grace's Alley, 1F 87 *Tower Hill*
Wyndham's, Charing Cross Road.1B 82 *Leicester Square*
Young Vic, The Cut. 5A 84 *Waterloo*

* Outside Central London area mapped.

CONCERT HALLS

Nearest station shown in italics.

Barbican Hall, Silk Street. 2E 73 *Barbican, Moorgate*
Cadogan Hall, Sloane Terrace 4F 91 *Sloane Square*
Central Hall, Tothill Street. 1A 94 *St. James's Park*
Conway Hall, Red Lion Square. 2D 71 *Holborn*
Guildhall School of Music and Drama, Barbican.
    2E 73 *Barbican, Moorgate*
Kings Place, York Way. 1C 62 *King's Cross St Pancras*
Logan Hall, Institute of Education, 20 Bedford Way.
    1A 70 *Russell Square*
*LSO St. Lukes, Old Street, EC1 *Old Street*
Purcell Room, South Bank. 3E 83 *Waterloo*
Queen Elizabeth Hall, South Bank. 3E 83 *Waterloo*

Royal Albert Hall, Kensington Gore. 1F 89
    South Kensington
Royal College of Music, Prince Consort Road.
    2F 89 *South Kensington*
Royal Festival Hall, Belvedere Road, South Bank.
    4E 83 *Waterloo*
St. John's Smth Square, Smith Square. 3B 94 *Westminster*
Scala, 275 Pentonville Road, 3C 62
    King's Cross St Pancras
*The O2 Arena, Peninsular Square, SE10.
    North Greenwich
*Wembley Arena, Empire Way, Wembley.
    Wembley Park
Wigmore Hall, 36 Wigmore Street. *4B 68 Bond Street.*
    Oxford Circus

* Outside Central London area mapped.

SELECTED SHOPS

Debenhams – 5B 68
Fenwick – 1C 80
Fortnum and Mason – 3E 81
Foyle's – 5A 70
Habitat – 1D 81 / 2F 69
Hamleys –1D 81
Harrods – 2D 91
Harvey Nichols – 1E 91
Heals – 2F 69
House of Fraser –5B 68
House of Fraser Victoria –
    3E 93
John Lewis – 5C 68
Liberty – 5D 69
Mappin and Webb – 1E 81
Marks and Spencer
    (Marble Arch) – 5F 67
Marks and Spencer
    (Oxford Circus) – 5D 69
Peter Jones – 5E 91
St.Christopher's Place– 4A68
Selfridges – 5A 68
Thomas Neal's –5B70
Top Shop – 4D69
West London Silver Vaults –
    3F 71
Whiteleys Centre – 5B 64

GOVERNMENT OFFICES

Business, Innovation
    & Skills, Dept of – 2A94
Commonwealth Office –
    5B 82
Defence, Ministry of – 4C 82
Education
    Department of – 2A 94
Environment, Food & Rural
    Affairs, (Defra)
    Department of – 3B 94
Foreign Office – 5B 82
Home Office – 3A 94
Houses of Parliament –
    1C 94
Land Registry – 4E 71
Northern Ireland Office
    – 4B 94
Passport Office – 4C 92
Patent Office – 1A 84
Scottish Office – 5B 82
Transport
    Department of – 4A 94
Treasury – 5B 82
Welsh Office – 5B 82

AUCTIONEERS

Bonhams – 5B 68 & 2C 90
Christies – 3E 81 & 5F 89
Sotheby's – 1C 80
Spink – 2B 70

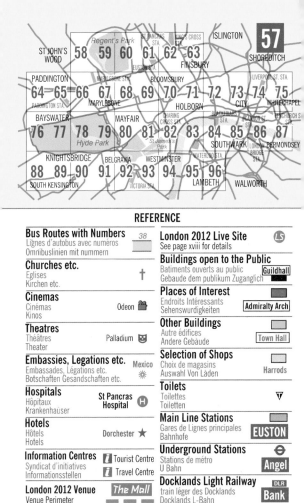

REFERENCE

Bus Routes with Numbers   38
Lignes d'autobus avec numéros
Omnibuslinien mit nummern

Churches etc.   †
Eglises
Kirchen etc.

Cinemas   Odeon 🎬
Cinémas
Kinos

Theatres   Palladium 🎭
Théâtres
Theater

Embassies, Legations etc.   Mexico
Embassades, Légations etc.   ☀
Botschaften Gesandschaften etc.

Hospitals   St Pancras
Hôpitaux   Hospital Ⓗ
Krankenhäuser

Hotels   Dorchester ★
Hôtels
Hotels

Information Centres   🛈 Tourist Centre
Syndicat d'initiatives
Informationsstellen   🛈 Travel Centre

London 2012 Venue   The Mall
Venue Perimeter

Scale: 1:10,560
6 inches to 1 mile

0	110	220 yards	¼ mile
0			500 metres

London 2012 Live Site   ⓁⓈ
See page xviii for details

Buildings open to the Public   Guildhall
Batiments ouverts au public
Gebaude dem publikum Zuganglich

Places of Interest   Admiralty Arch
Endroits Intéressants
Sehenswurdigkeiten

Other Buildings   Town Hall
Autre édifices
Andere Gebäude

Selection of Shops   Harrods
Choix de magasins
Auswahl Von Läden

Toilets   ▽
Toilettes
Toiletten

Main Line Stations   EUSTON
Gares de Lignes principales
Bahnhofe

Underground Stations   ⊖ Angel
Stations de métro
U Bahn

Docklands Light Railway   DLR Bank
train léger des Docklands
Docklands L-Bahn

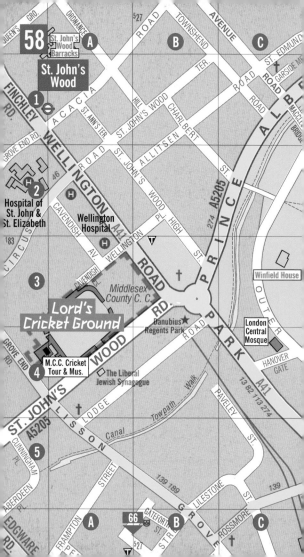

London Zoo

A

B ★York & Albany

C

PRINCE ALBERT ROAD

PARK-WAY

DELANCY ST.

ARLINGTON

529

274

ALBERT

MORNINGTON

VILLAGE

MORNINGTON

OUTER

GLOUCESTER GATE

A
L
B
A
N
Y

PARK

EAS

MO

AUB

1

Danish Church †

C2

Regent's Park Barracks

2

REGENT'S

CIRCLE

A4201

REDHILL ST.

Regent's †Park

59

183

Refreshments

PARK

Cumberland Gate

CUMBERLD. PK.

CHESTER

CUMBERLA

MARKET

3

St. John's Lodge

INNER

ROAD

ROBERT

Open Air

CIRCLE

CHESTER

▼

Chester Gate

TER.

CHESTER GATE

C2

S
T
R
E
E
T

4

▼

Queen Mary's Gardens

Westmir Kingsway

CIRCLE

reshments

INNER

5

Playground

Royal College of Physicians

LONGFORD

OSMABURGH

ST.

YORK BRIDGE

Melia White Ho.★

OSNABURGH TER.

N Dion

OUTER

CIRCLE

PARK WEST SQ.

PARK EAST SQ.

Great Port Street

YORK GA.

A

Music Mus.

68

Royal Academy of Music

NICK

30

▼

B **Regent's Park**

CR.

Royal National

E

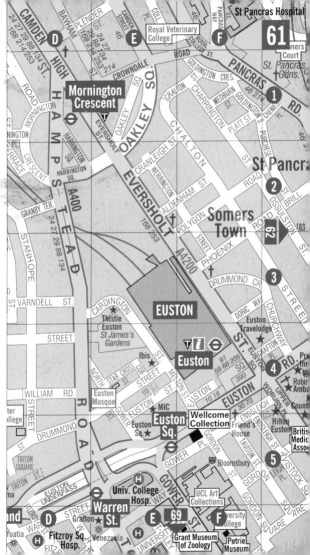

Cross

D

TREATY ST.
Union
Canal

CALEDONIAN ROAD A5203

EDONIAN RD.
CALSHOT

E

CARNEGIE ST.
17 91

MURIEL ST.
CHARLOTTE TER.

WYNFORD RD.

RODNEY ST.

Canal Tunnel

Elizabeth Garrett Anderson Language Coll.

RISINGHILL ST.

F

531 153 274

BARNSBURY RD.

COPENHAGEN ST.

CLOUDESLEY RD.

LIVERPOOL RD.

63

1

TOLPUDDLE ST.
153 274 394
MARKET

ROAD 153

PENTON ST.

CHAPEL ST.

BARON ST.

LION ST.

Eritrea
30 73 ☀

Pentonville

Mosque

COLLIER STREET

NORTHDOWN ST.

STREET

DONEGAL ST.

STREET

WHITE

STREET

LION

PENTONVILLE

KING'S

PENTON RISE

WESTON RISE

A501
30 73 205 214

CLAREMONT

AMWELL

ROAD

2

Jurys Inn ★

Crafts Council

The Angel Centre

SQUARE

MYDDELTON

83

3

Travelodge King's Cross
BRITANNIA ST.

SWINTON ST.

Royal National Throat, Nose & Ear Hosp.

H

Travelodge Royal Scott ★

PERCY CIRCUS

PERCY GT.

PERCY ST.

LLOYD ST.

LLOYD BAKER ST.

INGLEBERT ST.

RIVER ST.

Clerkenwell Magistrates Court

LLOYD SQUARE

GRAY'S

ACTON ST.

Arriva ★

CROSS ST.

CUBITT ST.

FREDERICK ST.

WHARTON ST.

Travelodge Farringdon ★

MARGERY ST.

HARDWICK ST.

4

Urdang Academy
Old Finsbury Town Hall

Clerkenwell

AV.

TYSOE ST.

ROSOMAN ST.

INN

A5200

SOUTH ST.

Kingsway Coll.
Inn Centre

MECKLENBURGH SQ.

Museum

Mecklenburgh Sq. Gdns.

Fields

Goodenough Club

GOUGH ST.

PHOENIX PL.

PAKENHAM ST.

CALTHORPE ST.

The Eastman Dental Hospital & Institute

H

Holiday Inn ★

FARRINGDON

Post Office
Mount Pleasant

British Postal Mus.
& Archive

London Metropolitan Archives

5

MT. MOUNT PLEASANT ST.

BOWLING GREEN LA.

ROSEBERY

63

AVE.

D

DOUGHTY ST.

MECKLENBURGH PL.

Grenville ST.

MILLMAN ST.

LAMB

E

The Charles Dickens Mus.

Independent Televis News

71 ▽

MT. PLEASANT

GRENVILLE M.

F

WARNER ST.

RAY ST.

531

ROAD

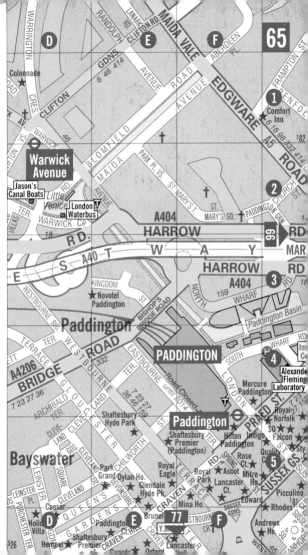

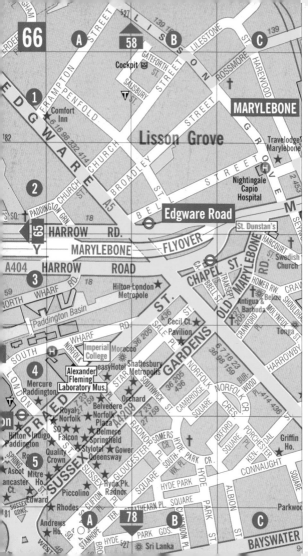

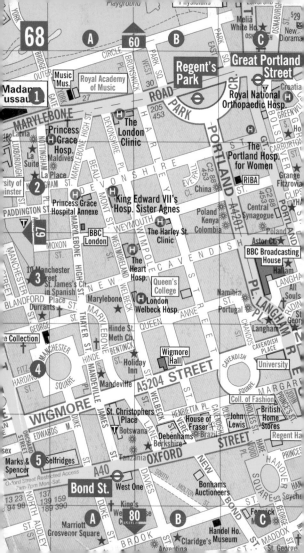

Mecklenburgh Sq. Gdns
Fields
Goodenough
Club
GRAY'S
CALTHORPE
GOUGH
MOUNT PLEASANT
PHŒNIX
531
D BURTON PL DOUGHTY ST **E** British Postal Mus. Archive **F** **71**
DOWLING
STREET
STREET
MILLMAN
DOUGHTY M
ST
Grenville
The Charles Dickens Mus.
Independent Television News
Pleasant
WARNER ST.
RAY ST.
FARRINGDON
BACK HILL
1
mond St. pital for ildren
ORMOND ST
ROGER
JOHN
RUGBY ST.
NORTHINGTON ST.
ROSEBERY
MOUNT
19 38 341
CLERKENWELL
ROAD
182
ROAD
HATTON
CROS
al London eopathic .
GT. JAMES
ST.
Malawi
Gray's Inn Gardens
55
London Weather Centre
17 45 46 341
LEATHER
2
Fa
DOMBEY ST
NEW
NORTH SQ
19 38 55 243
JOCKEY'S
BEDFORD
ROAD
Gray's Inn
DORRING-
TON ST.
LANE
72
ILLE
THEOBALD'S
Conway Hall
RED
PRINCETON
FIELDS
ROW
Hall
Library
ROAD
BROOKE ST.
LEATHER
LA.
GARDEN
Sierra Leone
LION
BRONNLOW
Chancery Lane
3 A40
ochrane 98
EAGLE
ST.
HOLBORN
INN
HOLBORN
FETTER
A4
CATTON
8 25 242 521
CHANCERY
West London Silver Vaults
STAPLE
STAPLE INN BDGS
FURNIVAL
NEW FETTER
LANE
Chancery Court
Sir John Soane's Museum
BREAM'S BLDGS
CURSITOR ST.
4
e Holborn
Lincoln's Inn Library Hall
Dr. Johns Hous
KING'S WAY
REMNANT
LINCOLN'S
Holborn
Lincoln's Inn Fields
Land Registry
King's College Library
579 768 ST.
Old Curiosity Shop
Royal College of Surgeons
SERLE
CAREY
Freemasons Hall
ngsway Hall
SARDINIA ST.
Hunterian Museum
Royal Courts of Justice
FETTER LA.
FLEET
ST.
5
3 26
Apex
KEMBLE
PORTUGAL
London School of Economics
ST.
FLEET ST.
4 11
BOUVERIE
 rf Hilton Novelli One Aldwych Duchess ME
Theatre Royal Drury Lane
Peacock
Temple Bar
Prince Henry's Room
Temple
Inner Temple
Hall
The Patent Office
Library
D
ALDWYCH
Bush House
India House
E
STRAND
Australia House
341
83
Two Temple Place
Hall Libr **F**
Middle Temple
The Temple
WELLIN
King's College

72

ROSEBERY AV.

BOWLING GRN. LA.
CLERKENWELL CL.
SEKFORDE ST.
ST. COMPTON ST.
DALLINGTON ST.
BERRY ST.
GOSW

The Newsroom Archives

A

B Finsbury

C

The Guardian

WARNER ST.

RAY ST.

The Clerk's Well

CLERKENWELL

AYLESBURY

GREAT SUTTON ST.

ROAD

19 38 341

1

BACK HILL

FARRINGDON LA.

VINE S. CLERKENWELL

Marx Memorial Library

CLERKENWELL GREEN

55 243

Zetter

ST. JOHN

Queen Mary Univ. of London (Charterhouse Campus)

182

LEATHER

HATTON

CLERKENWELL

FARRINGDON

TURNMILL

BRIT TON

St John's Gate

EAGLE

Charterhouse

ondon ther Centre

2

ST.

GARDEN

CROSS

ST.

COWCROSS

Farringdon

ST.

ST. JOHN ST.

Rookery ★

Malmaison

CHARTERHO SQ.

Fox & Anchor

Barbican

DORRIN

71

BROOKE

GREVILLE ST.

GARDEN

St Ethelreda's

ELY PL.

17
45 46

CHARTERHOUSE

STREET

LINDSEY

LONG

St. Ba the

3

STAPLE

FURNIVAL ST.

A40

HOLBORN

LEATHER LA.

HOLBORN CIR.

HOLBORN

FAR-

WEST

SMITHFIELD

Central Market (Smithfield)

WEST SMITHFIELD

LITTLE B

Museum

H

St. Bartholomew the Less

St. Bartholomew's Hospital

CURSITOR ST.

BREAM'S

4

NEW FETTER LANE

341

A4

ST. ANDREW STREET

SHOE LA.

City Temple

17 45 46

RINGDON ST.

ST. BRIDE ST.

STONE-CUTTER ST.

CITY (THAMESLINK)

8 17 25
242 521

St. Sepulchre

VIADUCT

BAILEY

NEWGATE

GUILTSPUR

56

Christchurc (Ruin)

King's College Library

Dr. Johnson's House

Ye Old Cheshire Cheese

Central Criminal Court (Old Bailey)

Stock Exchange

WARWICK LA.

AVE MARIA

Temple Bar Gate

FETTER LA.

LANE

FLEET

BOUVERIE ST.

WHITEFRIARS

5

Prince Henry's Room

Apex The Patent Office

1 15 23 26
76 172

St.

Bride's

STREET

LUDGATE

Stationers' Hall

Club Quarters

LUDGATE HILL

OLD

St Pa Cathe

Bar

Temple Hall

Inner Temple

Library

Crypt Mus.

St. Bride Foundation

SALISBURY

DORSET RISE

NEW BRI.

PILGRIM

CARTER

45 63 100

11 15 17 21 23 26
76 172

Apothecaries Hall

College o

A

The Temple

84

B Blackfriars

C

Grange (St. Paul's)

St. Andrew

QUE

388

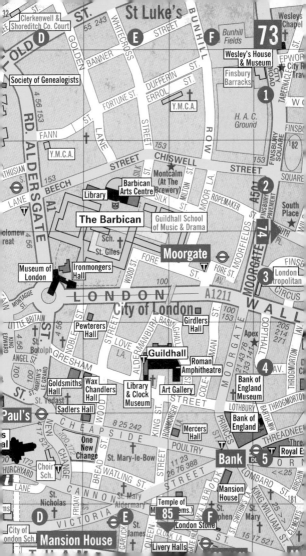

CITY
WESLEY'S CHAPEL
ST. LUKE STREET
74 B
C
Shoreditch
Wesley's House & Museum
Finsbury Barracks
1
City Road Travelodge
SCRUTTON ST.
HOLYWELL LA.
HIGH
SHOREDITCH
242 344 388
GREAT EASTERN STREET
HOLYWELL
EPWORTH ST.
TABERNACLE ST.
PAUL
SCRUTTON ST.
HOLYWELL ROW
SCRUTTON ST.
CURTAIN
NORTON FOLGATE
FOLGATE SQ.
WORSHIP STREET
H. A. C. Ground
FINSBURY
CHRISTOPHER ST.
PRIMROSE ST.
SPITAL
STREET
153
BAKER MEWS
APPOLD
Charnel House
A501
ROPEMAKER ST.
2
FINSBURY SQUARE
FINSBURY PAVEMENT
SUN ST.
CLIFTON ST.
ST.
STREET
182
SQUARE
South Place
St. Mary
BROADGATE CIRCLE
133 153
205 214 271
Broadgate Arena
8 26 35 42 47 48 78 135 149
Bishops Inst. &
BRUSHFIE
MOORGATE
73
SOUTH PL.
WILSON ST.
ELDON ST.
LIVERPOOL STREET
MIDDLESEX
Synagogue
Rav
FORE ST.
AV.
3
FINSBURY
London Metropolitan Uni.
BLOMFIELD ST.
LIVERPOOL
ANdAZ
i
Dirty Dicks
LONDON
A1211 WALL
CIRCUS
Liverpool St.
Liverpool St.
ANdAZ ST.
St. Botolph
Travelodge
100 153
205 214 271
COPTHALL
Apex
3 76 141
WORMWOOD STREET
Heron Tower
CAMOMILE ST.
CUTLER ST.
42 78 100
MOORGATE
AV.
Carpenters Hall
BROAD
Tower 42
St Ethelburga
BEVIS MARKS
Theatre
4
Bank of England Museum
THROGMORTON ST.
Dutch Church
Drapers Hall
+23
DPL
LOTHBURY
THROGMORTON ST.
OLD
St. Helens
Bevis Marks Synagogue
CREECHURCH LA.
42 78 100
205
Bank of England
BIRCHIN
BATHMAN
STREET
"The Gherkin"
St. Andrew
PRINCES
THREADNEEDLE
Merchant Taylors Hall
LEADENHALL
Lloyds Registry
Bank
5
Royal Exchange
Threadneedles
CORNHILL
<<25
Lloyds Building
STREET
BILLITER ST.
Mansion House
LOMBARD
ST.
St. Michael
Club Quarters
GRACECHURCH STREET
Leadenhall Market
FENCHURCH AV.
Cloth Workers Hall
FENCHU
St. Stephen
WALBROOK
ST. SWITHINS
KING WILLIAM ST.
St. Mary
A
86
FENCHURCH
B
C
tone
GREAT
15 17 521
PHILPOT LN.
OD LA.
St. Margaret
London
HART ST. CRUTCHED

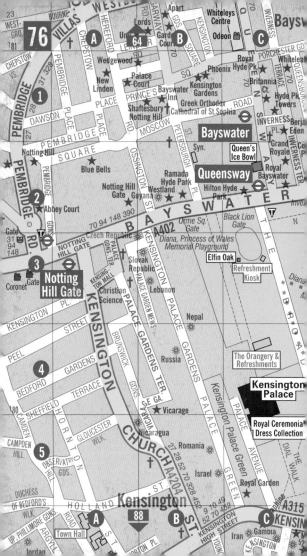

WEST-GRO 81
WEST-GRO
23
BOURNE
VILLAS
WESTBO
Apart
Lords
Whiteleys Centre
INVERNESS
Bays
CHEPSTOW VS.
CHEPSTOW
United
HEREFORD
Odeon
GARWAY
GDS
KENSINGTON
PORCHESTER GD
70
C
Whitele

Wedgewood
Garden
Court
SQUARE

New Linden
Palace Court
Phoenix
Hyde Pk
Royal
Queensborough TERRACE
Britannia
Ct.

PEMBRIDGE
28 31 328
PLACE
PRINCE'S
Bayswater
Inn
Kensington
Gardens
ROAD
INVERNESS
Hyde Pk Towers
Berja

1

27
DAWSON
PLACE
Shaftesbury
Notting Hill
Greek Orthodox
Cathedral of St.Sophia
Eden

PEMBRIDGE
PLACE
MOSCOW
PETERSBURGH
Bayswater
PL
Grand Royale
INVERNESS

SQUARE
Syn.
Queen's Ice Bowl
Royal Baltic

Notting Hill
Blue Bells
Ramada
Hyde Park
Queensway
Royal Baywater

2

PEMBRIDGE
Notting Hill
Gate
Guyana
Westland
Hilton Hyde
Park
B A Y S W A T E R
Inve

Abbey Court
BAYSWATER

Gate
31 94 148
70 94 148 390
A402
Orme Sq.
Gate
Black Lion Gate
N

Czech Republic
Diana, Princess of Wales Memorial Playground

3

NOTTING
HILL GATE
Slovak
Republic
Elfin Oak
Refreshment Kiosk
Diana

Coronet
Gate
Notting Hill Gate
Christian
Science
Lebanon

KENSINGTON
PEEL
Nepal
Russia
The Orangery & Refreshments

4

BEDFORD
GARDENS
TERRACE
BRUNSWICK
GDS
Kensington Palace

SHEFFIELD
HORNTON
PALACE GARDENS TER.
GE GA.
Vicarage
Royal Ceremonial Dress Collection

CAMPDEN
HILL
GLOUCESTER
WLK
Nicaragua

5

OBSERVATORY
GDS
CHURCH
A4204
27 28 52 70 328 452
Romania
Israel
Royal Garden

DUCHESS
OF BEDFORD'S
WLK
HOLLAND
Kensington
9 10 49
52 70 452
DIAL WALK
A315

PH. PHILLIMORE GDS
Town Hall
ST.
HIGH STREET
KENSINGTON HIGH STREET
Gambia
Iran
KENSIN

Jordan
NORTON PL.
Argyll

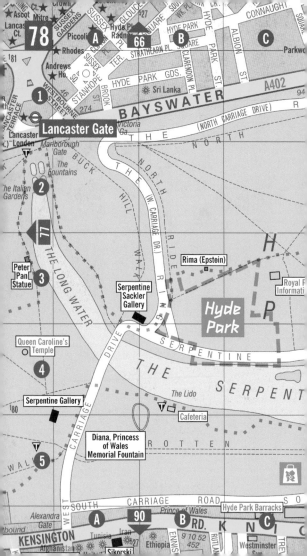

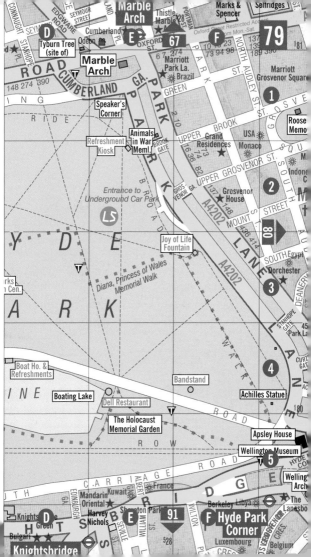

Marble Arch

Thistle
Marble

Marks &
Spencer

Selfridges

EDGWARE
SEYMOUR
STREET

Cumberland

67

Oxford Street Restricted Access
Mon-Sat.

79

CONNAUGHT

SEYMOUR

D
Tyburn Tree
(site of)

Odeon

E OXFORD
ST.

10
73 94 98

137
139
189

81

390

STANHOPE

PL.

**Marble
Arch**

67
274
Marriott
Park La.
Brazil

NORTH AUDLEY ST.

F

Marriott
Grosvenor Square

ROAD

CUMBERLAND

GA.

PARK

GREEN

ST.

1

148 274
390

Speaker's
Corner

PARK

BROOK

UPPER

Grand
Residences

USA

Monaco

ST.

GROSVENOR

Roose
Memo

RIDE

Refreshment
Kiosk

Animals
in War
Meml.

BROOK
GATE

UPPER GROSVENOR ST.

16 36 414
73

137

SQU

Indone

2

SOUTH

M

Entrance to
Underground Car Park

LS

GROS-
VENOR GA.

UPPER GROSVENOR ST.

Grosvenor
House

148

436 414

MOUNT STREET

STREET

80

HYDE

E

Joy of Life
Fountain

D

Diana, Princess of Wales
Memorial Walk

A4202

SOUTH Egypt

Dorchester

3

DEANERY

rks
n Cen.

PARK

4

LANE

WALK

STANHOPE
GATE

Park La

CURL
GAT

Boat Ho. &
Refreshments

Bandstand

Achilles Statue

AC

INE

Boating Lake

Dell Restaurant

The Holocaust
Memorial Garden

ROAD

ROW

Apsley House

HYDE

Wellington Museum

5

Welling
Arch

CARRIAGE

ROAD

BRIDGE

G

F

Wellin

D

Knights ge

Green

EDINBURGH GA.

Mandarin
Oriental

Kuwait

ALBERT

France

Berkeley Libya

E

The
Lanesbo

Bulgari

T

Harvey
Nichols

Sheraton Park

91

WILTON

**Hyde Park
Corner**

SEVILLE

WILLIAM

Knightsbridge

528

Luxembourg

CRES

Belgium

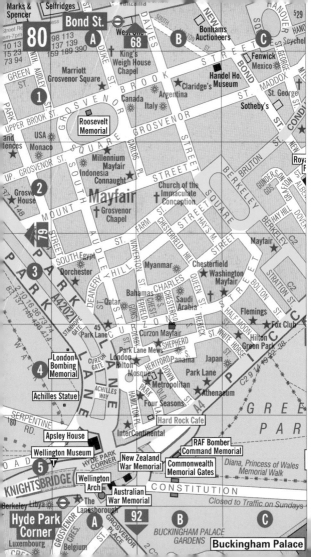

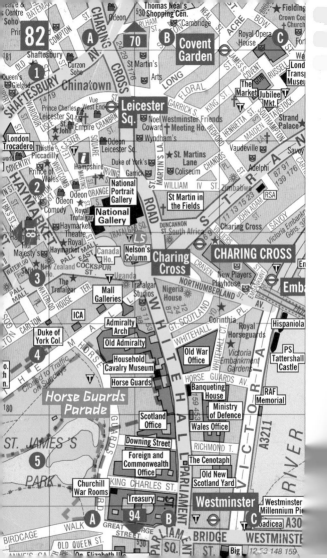

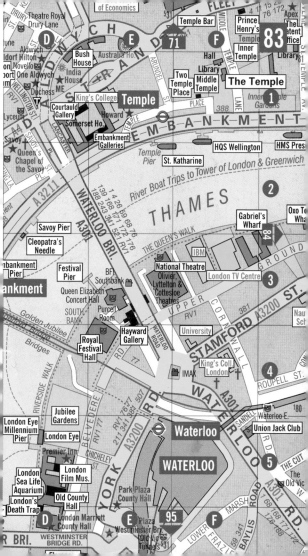

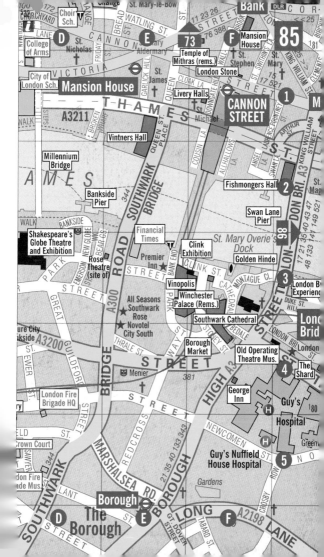

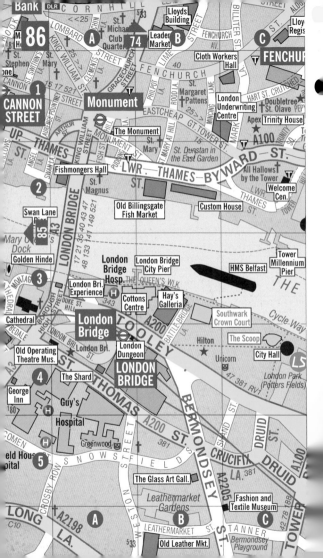

London Metropolitan
University

D hamberlain

Indigo

FRIARS
ST.

INDIA
ST.

MANSELL ST.

A1210

534

LEMAN ST.

75

CHURCH ST.

WALK

F ER ST.

ELLEN
ST.

181

E Grange

Mosque

CRUTCH ST.

CROSSWALL

PORTSOKEN ST.

Premier
Inn

PRESCOT
STREET

CABLE STREET

Novotel
ower Bri,
Trinity Sq
Gardens

Cooper's
Grange
City

Travelodge

DLR

Tower Gateway

Tower Hill

SHORTER ST.

ROYAL MINT ST.

CHAMBER STREET

Travelodge

GOODMANS
YARD
RV1

1 Wiltons
Music Hall

DOCK ST.
A1202

CARTWRIGHT ST.

THE HIGHWAY

Tower
Gdns.

15

Old Royal
Mint

EAST SMITHFIELD

A1203

THOMAS MORE ST.

VAUGHAN WAY

2

TOWER HILL

TOWER BRIDGE APPROACH

**The Tower of
London**

ST. KATHARINE'S WAY

St Katharine Docks
& Yacht Haven

KENNET ST.

3

Tower Bridge
Exhibition

A100

TOWER BRIDGE

RV1 42 78

Tower

St. Katharine's
Pier

SAINT KATHARINE'S MEWS

WAY

WAPPING HIGH ST.

WAY

4

POOL

River Boat Trips to Greenwich

Tower Bridge
Wharf

180

Bridge
Engine Room

SHAD THAMES

Anchor Brewhouse

HORSELYDOWN LA.

GAINSFORD ST.

Butlers
Wharf

Tower Bridge
Piazza

Design
Museum

Magistrates Court

Camera Press
Gallery

MAGUIRE ST.

SHAD THAMES ST.

Dock

5

QNE

LAFONE ST.

ELIZABETH ST.

188 381

47

A200

SHAD THAMES

Bermondsey

BERMONDSEY
WALL WEST

GEORGE RW.

CHAMBERS

A2207

D TANNER
ST.

STREET

A200

E MILL ST.

JAMAICA
RD.

WOLSELEY ST.

F

534

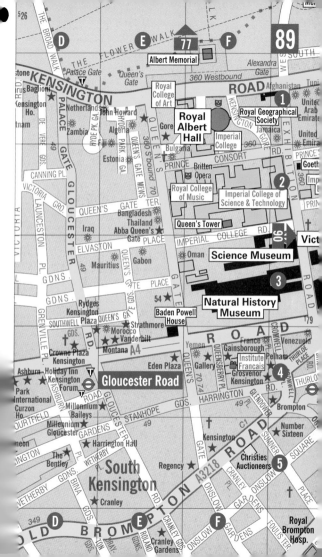

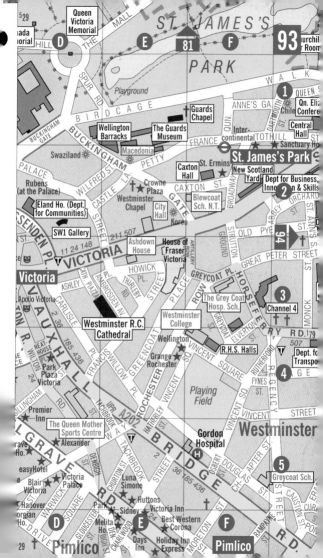

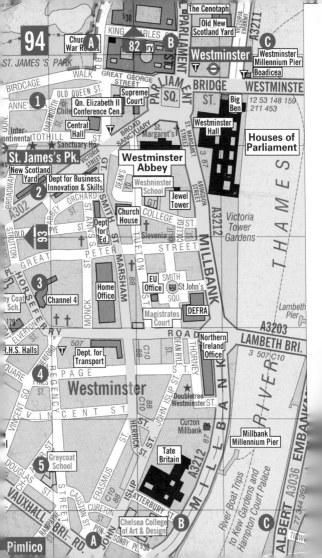

94

St. James's Park

Churchill War Rooms — **A**

KING CHARLES ST

82 Treasury — **B**

GREAT GEORGE STREET

BIRDCAGE WALK

ANNE'S GATE

OLD QUEEN ST.

1

DARTMOUTH ST

Inter-continental

TOTHILL

Sanctuary Ho.

Qn. Elizabeth II Conference Cen.

Chile

Supreme Court

Central Hall

BROAD SANCTUARY

St. Margaret's

St. James's Pk.

New Scotland Yard

2 Dept for Business, Innovation & Skills

VICTORIA STREET

DEAN'S YD.

Westminster Abbey

ABBEY ORCHARD ST.

ST. ANN'S ST.

PYE

93

STROLD

ST. ANN'S ST.

Dept for Ed.

Westminster School

Church House

Slovenia

Jewel Tower

COLLEGE

The Cenotaph

Old New Scotland Yard

VICTORIA EMBANKMENT

A3211

C

Westminster

Westminster Millennium Pier

Boadicea

PARLIAMENT ST

BRIDGE WESTMINSTER

PARLIAMENT SQ.

WESTMINSTER ST.

Big Ben

12 53 148 159 211 453

Houses of Parliament

Westminster Hall

3 87

ST. MARGARET STREET

ABINGDON STREET

Victoria Tower Gardens

A3212

THAMES

BROAD SANCTUARY

GT. PETER STREET

MARSHAM ST.

TUFTON STREET

MILLBANK

Home Office

3

Grey Coat Sch.

Channel 4

HORSEFERRY

179

MONCK ST.

EU Office

St John's SQU.

SMITH SQ.

DEFRA

Magistrates Court

Lambeth Pier

A3203

R.H.S. Halls

ELVERTON ST.

HERFORD ST.

507

Dept. for Transport

REGENCY ST.

PAGE ST.

Northern Ireland Office

ROAD

LAMBETH BRI.

3 507 C10

SQUARE

VINCENT SQ.

ETHOS ST.

4

Westminster

VINCENT STREET

C10 88

DEAN RYLE ST.

JOHN ISLIP ST.

THORNEY ST.

Doubletree Westminster ST.

Curzon Millbank

Millbank Millennium Pier

DOUGLAS ST.

CHS.

5

Greycoat School

ERASMUS ST.

HERRICK ST.

ISLIP ST.

Tate Britain

A3212

MILLBANK

River Boat Trips to Kew Gardens and Hampton Court Palace

ALBERT EMBANKMENT

A3036

RIVER

VAUXHALL BRI.

RAMPAYNE ST.

CAUSTON ST.

CURETON ST.

PONSONBY

JOHN ISLIP ST.

SATTERBURY ST.

Chelsea College of Art & Design

A

SONBY PL

530

B

TfL 344 360

C

Pimlico

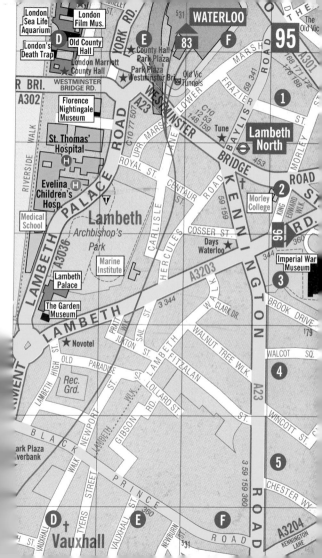

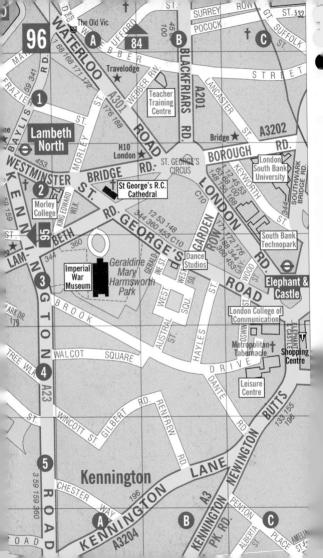

Abbreviations:

All : Alley
App : Approach
Arc : Arcade
Av : Avenue
Bk : Back
Boulevd : Boulevard
Bri : Bridge
B'way : Broadway
Bldgs : Buildings
Bus : Business
Cen : Centre
Chu : Church
Chyd : Churchyard
Circ : Circle
Cir : Circus
Clo : Close
Comn : Common
Cotts : Cottages

Ct : Court
Cres : Crescent
Dri : Drive
E : East
Embkmt : Embankment
Est : Estate
Gdns : Gardens
Ga : Gate
Gt : Great
Grn : Green
Gro : Grove
Ho : House
Ind : Industrial
Junct : Junction
La : Lane
Lit : Little
Lwr : Lower
Mnr : Manor
Mans : Mansions
Mkt : Market

M : Mews
Mt : Mount
N : North
Pal : Palace
Pde : Parade
Pk : Park
Pas : Passage
Pl : Place
Rd : Road
S : South
Sq : Square
Sta : Station
St : Street
Ter : Terrace
Up : Upper
Vs : Villas
Wlk : Walk
W : West
Yd : Yard

Hanover St. W1 —5C 68
Hans Cres. SW1 —2D 91
Hanson St. W1 —2D 69
Hans Pl. SW1 —3E 91
Hans Rd. SW3 —2D 91
Hans St. SW1 —3E 91
Harcourt St. W1 —3C 66
Hardwick St. EC1 —4F 63
Harewood Av. NW1 —1C 66
Harewood Pl. W1 —5C 68
Harley St. W1 —1B 68
Harrington Gdns. SW7 —5C 88
Harrington Rd. SW7 —4F 89
Harrington Sq. NW1 —2D 61
Harrowby St. W1 —4C 66
Harrow Pl. E1 —4C 74
Harrow Rd. W9 —1A 64
Harrow Rd. W2 —3B 64
Hart St. EC3 —1C 86
Hasker St. SW3 —4C 90
Hastings St. WC1 —4B 62
Hatfields. SE1 —3A 84
Hatherley St. SW1 —5E 93
Hatton Garden. EC1 —2A 72
Hay Hill. W1 —2C 80
Hayles St. SE11 —4B 96
Haymarket. SW1 —2F 81
Hayne St. EC1 —2C 72
Hay's M. W1 —2B 80
Henrietta Pl. W1 —4B 68
Henrietta St. WC2 —1C 82
Herbert Cres. SW1 —2E 91
Herbrand St. WC1 —5B 62
Hercules Rd. SE1 —3E 95
Herrick St. SW1 —5A 94
Hertford Rd. W2 —4A 64
Hertford St. W1 —4B 80
High Holborn. WC1 —4C 70
Highway, The. E1 —2F 87
Hill St. W1 —3A 80
Hinde St. W1 —4A 68
Hobart Pl. SW1 —2B 92
Hogarth Rd. SW5 —5B 88
Holbein Pl. SW1 —5F 91
Holborn. EC1 —3F 71
Holborn Cir. EC1 —3A 72
Holborn Viaduct. EC1 —3B 72
Holland St. SE1 —3C 84
Holland St. W8 —1A 88
Holles St. W1 —4C 68
Holywell La. EC2 —1C 74
Holywell Row. EC2 —1B 74
Homer Row. W1 —3C 66
Hooper St. E1 —5F 75
Hopton St. SE1 —3C 84
Hornton St. W8 —5A 76
Horseferry Rd. SW1 —4F 93
Horseguards Av. SW1 —4B 82
Horse Guards Rd. SW1 —4A 82

Horselydown La. SE1 —5D 87
Horton Pl. W8 —1A 88
Houndsditch. EC3 —4C 74
Howick Pl. SW1 —3E 93
Howland St. W1 —2E 69
Hugh St. SW1 —5C 92
Hunter St. WC1 —5C 62
Huntley St. WC1 —1E 69
Hyde Pk. Corner W1 —5A 80
Hyde Pk. Cres. W2 —5B 66
Hyde Pk. Gdns. W2 —1A 78
Hyde Pk. Ga. SW7 —1E 89
(in two parts)
Hyde Pk. Sq. W2 —5B 66
Hyde Pk. St. W2 —5B 66

Imperial College Rd. SW7 —3F 89
India St. EC3 —5D 75
Inglebert St. EC1 —3F 63
Inner Circ. NW1 —4F 59
Inverness Pl. W2 —1C 76
Inverness Ter. W2 —5C 64
Ironmonger La. EC2 —5E 73
Irving St. WC2 —2A 82
Ivor Pl. NW1 —1D 67
Ixworth Pl. SW3 —5B 90

Jamaica Rd. SE1 —5E 87
James St. W1 —5A 68
James St. WC2 —1C 82
Jermyn St. SW1 —3D 81
Jewry St. EC3 —5D 75
Jockey's Fields. WC1 —2E 71
John Adam St. WC2 —2C 82
John Islip St. SW1 —5A 94
John Prince's St. W1 —4C 68
John St. WC1 —1E 71
Joiner St. SE1 —4A 86
Judd St. WC1 —4B 62
Juxton St. SE11 —4E 95

Kemble St. WC2 —5D 71
Kendal St. W2 —5C 66
Kennet St. E1 —3F 87
Kennington La. SE11 —5A 96
Kennington Pk. Rd. SE11 —5B 96
Kennington Rd. SE1 & SE11
—2F 95
Kensington Chu. St. W8 —3A 76
Kensington Ct. W8 —1C 88
Kensington Ct. Pl. W8 —2C 88
Kensington Gdns. Sq. W2 —5B 64
Kensington Gore. SW7 —1F 89
Kensington High St. W8 —2A 88
Kensington Mall. W8 —3A 76
Kensington Pal. Gdns. W8 —3B 76
Kensington Pl. W8 —3A 76
Kensington Rd. SW7 —1D 89

Kensington Sq. W8 —2B 88
Keyworth St. SE1 —2C 96
King Charles St. SW1 —5A 82
Kingdom St. W2 —3E 65
King Edward St. EC1 —4D 73
King Edward Wlk. SE1 —2A 96
Kingly St. W1 —5D 69
King's Boulevd. NW1 —2B 62
King's Rd. SW3 —5D 91
King's Cross Rd. WC1 —3D 63
King St. EC2 —4E 73
King St. SW1 —4E 81
King St. WC2 —1B 82
Kingsway. WC2 —4D 71
King William St. EC4 —5A 74
Knaresborough Pl. SW5 —4B 88
Knightsbridge. SW7 & SW1
—1C 90

Lafone St. SE1 —5D 87
Lambeth Bri. SW1 & SE1 —4C 94
Lambeth High St. SE1 —4D 95
Lambeth Pal. Rd. SE1 —3D 95
Lambeth Rd. SE1 —3D 95
Lambeth Wlk. SE11 —4E 95
(in two parts)
Lamb's Conduit St. WC1 —1D 71
Lamb St. E1 —2D 75
Lanark Rd. W9 —1E 65
Lancaster Ga. W2 —2D 77
Lancaster Pl. WC2 —1D 83
Lancaster St. SE1 —1B 96
Lancaster Ter. W2 —1F 77
Lancaster Wlk. W2 —3E 77
Lancelot Pl. SW7 —1D 91
Langham Pl. W1 —3C 68
Langham St. W1 —3C 68
Lansdowne Ter. WC1 —5C 62
Lant St. SE1 —5D 85
Launceston Pl. W8 —2D 89
Laurence Pountney St. EC4
—1F 85
Laverton Pl. SW5 —5C 88
Lavington St. SE1 —4C 84
Leadenhall St. EC3 —5B 74
Leather La. EC1 —2F 71
(in two parts)
Leathermarket St. SE1 —5B 86
Leicester Sq. WC2 —2A 82
Leigh St. WC1 —4B 62
Leinster Gdns. W2 —5D 65
Leinster Pl. W2 —5D 65
Leinster Sq. W2 —5A 64
Leinster Ter. W2 —2D 77
Leman St. E1 —4B 75
Lennox Gdns. SW1 —3D 91
Leonard St. EC2 —1A 74
Lexham Gdns. W8 —4A 88
Lexington St. W1 —1E 81
Lilestone St. NW8 —5B 58

Lime St. EC3 —1B 86
Lincoln's Inn Fields. WC2 —4D 71
Lindsey St. EC1 —2C 72
Lisle St. WC2 —1A 82
Lisson Gro. NW8 & NW1 —5A 58
Lit. Britain. EC1 —3C 72
Lit. College Street. SW1 —2B 94
Liverpool Rd. N1 —1F 63
Liverpool St. EC2 —3B 74
Lloyd Baker St. WC1 —4F 63
Lloyd Sq. WC1 —3F 63
Lloyd St. WC1 —3F 63
Lodge Rd. NW8 —4A 58
Logan Pl. W8 —4A 88
Lollard St. SE11 —4E 95
Lombard St. EC3 —5A 74
London Bri. SE1 & EC4 —3A 86
London Bri. St. SE1 —4A 86
London Rd. SE1 —2B 96
London St. W2 —4F 65
London Wall. EC2 —3E 73
Long Acre. WC2 —1B 82
Longford St. NW1 —5C 60
Long La. EC1 —2C 72
Long La. SE1 —5F 85
Lord Hills Bri. W2 —3B 64
Lothbury. EC2 —4F 73
Love La. EC2 —4E 73
Lwr. Belgrave St. SW1 —3B 92
Lwr. Grosvenor Pl. SW1 —2C 92
Lwr. James St. W1 —1E 81
Lwr. John St. W1 —1E 81
Lwr. Marsh. SE1 —1F 95
Lwr. Sloane St. SW1 —5B 91
Lwr. Thames St. EC3 —2A 86
Lowndes Sq. SW1 —1E 91
Lowndes St. SW1 —2F 91
Ludgate Cir. EC4 —5B 72
Ludgate Hill. EC4 —5B 72
Luke St. EC2 —1B 74
Luxborough St. W1 —2F 67
Lyall St. SW1 —3F 9

Mabledon Pl. WC1 —4A 62
Macclesfield Bri. NW1 —1C 58
Macklin St. WC2 —4C 70
Maddox St. W1 —1C 80
Maguire St. SE1 —5E 87
Maida Av. W2 —2E 65
Maida Vale. W9 —1E 65
Maiden La. WC2 —1C 82
Malet St. WC1 —1F 69
Mall, The. SW1 —4A 82
Manchester Sq. W1 —4A 68
Manchester St. W1 —3F 67
Mandeville Pl. W1 —4A 68
Manningtree St. E1 —4F 75
Mansell St. E1 —5E 75
Maple St. W1 —2D 69

Portman St. W1 —5F 67
Portsoken St. E1 —1E 87
Portugal St. WC2 —5E 71
Poultry. EC2 —5F 73
Praed St. W2 —4F 65
Pratt Wlk. SE11 —4E 95
Prescot St. E1 —1E 87
Primrose St. EC2 —2B 74
Prince Albert Rd. NW8 & NW1
(in two parts) —3B 58
Prince Consort Rd. SW7 —2E 89
Prince's Gdns. SW7 —2A 90
(in two parts)
Prince's Sq. W2 —1B 76
Prince's St. EC2 —5F 73
Princes St. W1 —5C 68
Princeton St. WC1 —2D 71
Procter St. WC1 —3D 71
Pudding La. EC3 —2A 86
Puddle Dock. EC4 —1C 84
Purchese St. NW1 —2A 62

Quaker St. E1 —1D 75
Queen Anne's Ga. SW1 —1F 93
Queen Anne St. W1 —3B 68
Queen Elizabeth St. SE1 —5D 87
Queensberry Pl. SW7 —4F 89
Queensborough Ter. W2 —1C 76
Queen's Gdns. W2 —1D 77
Queen's Ga. SW7 —1E 89
Queen's Ga. Gdns. SW7 —3E 89
Queen's Ga. M. SW7 —2E 89
Queen's Ga. Pl. SW7 —3E 89
Queen's Ga. Ter. SW7 —2E 89
Queen's Gro. NW8 —1A 58
Queen Sq. WC1 —1C 70
Queen St. EC4 —1E 85
Queen St. W1 —3B 80
Queen St. Pl. EC4 —2E 85
Queen's Wlk. SW1 —4D 81
Queensway. W2 —4C 64
Queen Victoria St. EC4 —1B 84

Radnor Pl. W2 —5B 66
Rampayne St. SW1 —5F 93
Randolph Av. W9 —1E 65
Ranelagh Bri. W2 —3C 64
Rathbone Pl. W1 —3F 69
Rathbone St. W1 —3E 69
Rawlings St. SW3 —5D 91
Ray St. EC1 —1A 72
Redchurch St. E2 —1D 75
Redcross Way. SE1 —5E 85
Redhill St. NW1 —2C 60
Red Lion Sq. WC1 —3D 71
Red Lion St. WC1 —2D 71
Regency St. SW1 —4F 93
Regent Sq. WC1 —4C 62

Regent St. W1 —4C 68
Regent St. SW1 —2F 81
Remnant St. WC2 —4D 71
Renfrew Rd. SE11 —4B 96
Richmond Ter. SW1 —5B 82
Riding Ho. St. W1 —3C 68
Ring, The. W2 —3B 78
Risinghill St. N1 —2E 63
Riverside Wlk. EC4 —1C 83
Riverside Wlk. SE1 —2D 95
River St. EC1 —3F 63
Robert St. NW1 —4C 60
Rochester Row. SW1 —4E 93
Rodney St. N1 —1E 63
Roger St. WC1 —1E 71
Roland Gdns. SW7 —5E 89
Rood La. EC3 —1B 86
Ropemaker St. EC2 —2F 73
Rosebery Av. EC1 —1F 71
Rossmore Rd. NW1 —1C 66
Rotten Row. SW7 & SW1 —5A 78
Roupell St. SE1 —4A 84
Royal College St. NW1 —1F 61
Royal Mint St. E1 —1F 87
Royal St. SE1 —2E 95
Rugby St. WC1 —1D 71
Rupert St. W1 —1F 81
Russell Sq. WC1 —2B 70
Russell St. WC2 —1C 82
Rutherford St. SW1 —4F 93
Rutland St. SW7 —2C 90

Sackville St. W1 —2D 81
Sail St. SE11 —4E 95
St Albans Gro. W8 —2C 88
St Alban's St. SW1 —2F 81
St Andrew St. EC4 —3A 72
St Ann's St. SW1 —2A 94
St Ann's Ter. NW8 —1A 58
St Barnabas St. SW1 —5A 92
St Botolph St. EC3 —4D 75
St Bride St. EC4 —4B 72
St Christopher's Pl. W1 —4A 68
St Cross St. EC1 —2A 72
St Edmund's Ter. NW8 —1C 58
St George's Cir. SE1 —2B 96
St George's Dri. SW1 —5C 92
St George's Rd. SE1 —2A 96
St George St. W1 —1C 80
St Giles Cir. W1 —4A 70
St Giles High St. WC2 —4A 70
St James's Pl. SW1 —4D 81
St James's Sq. SW1 —3E 81
St James's St. SW1 —3E 81
St John La. EC1 —2B 72
St John St. EC1 —1B 72
St John's Wood High St. NW8 —2A 58

INDEX TO EMBASSIES, LEGATIONS AND COMMONWEALTH REPRESENTATIVES

INDEX TO HOSPITALS